DIAGNOSING ORGANIZATIONS

Second Edition

Applied Social Research Methods Series
Volume 8

APPLIED SOCIAL RESEARCH METHODS SERIES

1. **SURVEY RESEARCH METHODS (Second Edition)** by FLOYD J. FOWLER, Jr.
2. **INTEGRATING RESEARCH (Second Edition)** by HARRIS M. COOPER
3. **METHODS FOR POLICY RESEARCH** by ANN MAJCHRZAK
4. **SECONDARY RESEARCH (Second Edition)** by DAVID W. STEWART and MICHAEL A. KAMINS
5. **CASE STUDY RESEARCH (Second Edition)** by ROBERT K. YIN
6. **META-ANALYTIC PROCEDURES FOR SOCIAL RESEARCH (Revised Edition)** by ROBERT ROSENTHAL
7. **TELEPHONE SURVEY METHODS (Second Edition)** by PAUL J. LAVRAKAS
8. **DIAGNOSING ORGANIZATIONS (Second Edition)** by MICHAEL I. HARRISON
9. **GROUP TECHNIQUES FOR IDEA BUILDING (Second Edition)** by CARL M. MOORE
10. **NEED ANALYSIS** by JACK McKILLIP
11. **LINKING AUDITING AND METAEVALUATION** by THOMAS A. SCHWANDT and EDWARD S. HALPERN
12. **ETHICS AND VALUES IN APPLIED SOCIAL RESEARCH** by ALLAN J. KIMMEL
13. **ON TIME AND METHOD** by JANICE R. KELLY and JOSEPH E. McGRATH
14. **RESEARCH IN HEALTH CARE SETTINGS** by KATHLEEN E. GRADY and BARBARA STRUDLER WALLSTON
15. **PARTICIPANT OBSERVATION** by DANNY L. JORGENSEN
16. **INTERPRETIVE INTERACTIONISM** by NORMAN K. DENZIN
17. **ETHNOGRAPHY (Second Edition)** by DAVID M. FETTERMAN
18. **STANDARDIZED SURVEY INTERVIEWING** by FLOYD J. FOWLER, Jr. and THOMAS W. MANGIONE
19. **PRODUCTIVITY MEASUREMENT** by ROBERT O. BRINKERHOFF and DENNIS E. DRESSLER
20. **FOCUS GROUPS** by DAVID W. STEWART and PREM N. SHAMDASANI
21. **PRACTICAL SAMPLING** by GARY T. HENRY
22. **DECISION RESEARCH** by JOHN S. CARROLL and ERIC J. JOHNSON
23. **RESEARCH WITH HISPANIC POPULATIONS** by GERARDO MARIN and BARBARA VANOSS MARIN
24. **INTERNAL EVALUATION** by ARNOLD J. LOVE
25. **COMPUTER SIMULATION APPLICATIONS** by MARCIA LYNN WHICKER and LEE SIGELMAN
26. **SCALE DEVELOPMENT** by ROBERT F. DeVELLIS
27. **STUDYING FAMILIES** by ANNE P. COPELAND and KATHLEEN M. WHITE
28. **EVENT HISTORY ANALYSIS** by KAZUO YAMAGUCHI
29. **RESEARCH IN EDUCATIONAL SETTINGS** by GEOFFREY MARUYAMA and STANLEY DENO
30. **RESEARCHING PERSONS WITH MENTAL ILLNESS** by ROSALIND J. DWORKIN
31. **PLANNING ETHICALLY RESPONSIBLE RESEARCH** by JOAN E. SIEBER
32. **APPLIED RESEARCH DESIGN** by TERRY E. HEDRICK, LEONARD BICKMAN, and DEBRA J. ROG
33. **DOING URBAN RESEARCH** by GREGORY D. ANDRANOVICH and GERRY RIPOSA
34. **APPLICATIONS OF CASE STUDY RESEARCH** by ROBERT K. YIN
35. **INTRODUCTION TO FACET THEORY** by SAMUEL SHYE and DOV ELIZUR with MICHAEL HOFFMAN
36. **GRAPHING DATA** by GARY T. HENRY
37. **RESEARCH METHODS IN SPECIAL EDUCATION** by DONNA M. MERTENS and JOHN A. McLAUGHLIN
38. **IMPROVING SURVEY QUESTIONS** by FLOYD J. FOWLER, Jr.
39. **DATA COLLECTION AND MANAGEMENT** by MAGDA STOUTHAMER-LOEBER and WELMOET BOK VAN KAMMEN
40. **MAIL SURVEYS** by THOMAS W. MANGIONE
41. **QUALITATIVE RESEARCH DESIGN** by JOSEPH A. MAXWELL
42. **ANALYZING COSTS, PROCEDURES, PROCESSES, AND OUTCOMES IN HUMAN SERVICES** by BRIAN T. YATES
43. **DOING LEGAL RESEARCH** by ROBERT A. MORRIS, BRUCE D. SALES, and DANIEL W. SHUMAN
44. **RANDOMIZED EXPERIMENTS FOR PLANNING AND EVALUATION** by ROBERT F. BORUCH
45. **MEASURING COMMUNITY INDICATORS** by PAUL J. GRUENEWALD, ANDREW J. TRENO, GAIL TAFF, and MICHAEL KLITZNER

DIAGNOSING ORGANIZATIONS

Methods, Models, and Processes

Second Edition

Michael I. Harrison

Applied Social Research Methods Series
Volume 8

SAGE Publications
International Educational and Professional Publisher
Thousand Oaks London New Delhi

For information address:

SAGE Publications, Inc.
2455 Teller Road
Thousand Oaks, California 91320
E-mail:order@sagepub.com

SAGE Publications Ltd.
6 Bonhill Street
London EC2A 4PU
United Kingdom

SAGE Publications India Pvt. Ltd.
M-32 Market
Greater Kailash I
New Delhi 110 048 India

Printed in the United States of America

Library of Congress Cataloging-in-Publication Data

Harrison, Michael I.
Diagnosing organizations: methods, models, and processes / Michael I. Harrison.—2nd ed.
p. cm.—(Applied social research methods series; v. 8)
Includes bibliographical references and index.
ISBN 0-8039-5644-4.—ISBN 0-8039-5645-2 (pbk.)
1. Organizational behavior. 2. Organizational change. I. Title. II. Series.
HD58.7.H3697 1994
302.3′5—dc20 93-47334

97 98 99 00 01 10 9 8 7

Sage Production Editor: Rebecca Holland

Contents

Preface

This book introduces organizational diagnosis to readers who have a basic knowledge of methods and concepts in the social and behavioral sciences but limited exposure to the fields of organizational behavior and consulting for organizational change. Organizational diagnosis involves using conceptual models and methods from the social and behavioral sciences to assess an organization's current state and to find ways to solve specific problems or increase effectiveness. Diagnosis can thus guide both organizational consulting and managerial decision making and planning. Diagnosis can help managers and consultants decide how to cope with crises or accomplish a major transition, such as a merger or a change of strategy. Diagnosis can also aid the pursuit of more modest objectives, such as improvements in quality or customer service.

Since the original edition of this book, which was written nearly a decade ago, major changes have occurred in the applications of the social and behavioral sciences to management and planned organizational change. Traditional organization development approaches, which envisioned a broad role for consultants in planning and introducing change, have given way to management-driven efforts to enhance human resource management and sometimes to achieve organizational renewals or transformations. The uses and approaches of diagnosis have also changed in response to these developments.

While preserving the format and length of the original book, I have rewritten this revised edition to reflect these new uses of diagnosis. Moreover, I have adopted a contemporary approach to planned organizational change and effectiveness that is gradually supplanting the views of traditional organization development. This newer approach includes four main elements:

1. Macro-organizational forces, such as organizational structure, technology, environmental relations, strategy, and culture, greatly affect organizational change and effectiveness.
2. Power alignments and political bargaining in and around organizations play a crucial role in organizational consultation and planned change.

3. Managerial and consultant roles in planned change necessarily vary across the organizational life cycle and are shaped by an organization's overall state of growth, decline, or crisis.
4. Consultants can facilitate major organizational changes and transformations, but managers typically drive them.

In addition to making revisions designed to reflect this approach, I have updated the discussion of the impacts of job design on performance and have added a discussion of the contributions of diagnosis to the management of mergers and strategic alliances between organizations. In keeping with current views about quality improvement and the need for organizations to satisfy multiple constituencies, I have placed greater stress on directly assessing the ways that clients and other external groups view an organization's products or services and judge its effectiveness. Moreover, I have further emphasized the importance of understanding and examining divergences of interests and interpretations among organizational subgroups. Within the limits imposed by the format of the series, I have also given more attention to assessing the impacts of organizational culture on work processes and organization-environment relations. In addition, I have rewritten the opening and concluding chapters to highlight the factors that contribute to successful diagnosis and the professional and ethical dilemmas facing practitioners of diagnosis.

The appendices and references to diagnostic instruments throughout the text now provide information about several new diagnostic instruments and the current status of older instruments that continue to be very useful. New cases have been added to illustrate the uses of diagnosis in a wide range of projects and types of organizations.

A short book cannot cover all of the topics important to practitioners of diagnosis. The choice of material becomes all the more difficult as the field of organizational studies branches out in many directions and moves far away from the immediate concerns of behavioral science practitioners. To help bridge the growing gap between researchers and practitioners, Aryeh Shirom and I are writing an advanced book on models for organizational diagnosis and assessment, also to be published by Sage.

My students at Bar-Ilan University and at Boston College contributed significantly to this project through their course participation and reports on organizations in which they worked and conducted research. I also appreciate the feedback that I received from many managers and consultants who participated in workshops on diagnosis and change that

I conducted in Holland and Israel. Yaacov Ben Dor, the head of the consulting firm TIL, Nissan Hadas, and Izik Uno of the Israel Air Force provided opportunities to engage in diagnostic work, to help other practitioners build their skills, and to develop my own approach to diagnosis and consulting. Among the people who generously shared their consulting experiences with me and discussed issues raised in this book were Sarah Edom, Ephraim Golan, and other members of the Kibbutz Industries Organizational Consulting Unit; Jan Jonker, of JAB Management Consultants and the University of Nijmegen; Bruce Phillips, formerly of General Motors and now a consultant and colleague at Bar-Ilan; Yizhak Samuel and Moshe Stillerman of Rafael; and my wife, Jo-Ann Harrison, of Bar-Ilan's School of Education.

The groundwork for the first edition of the book was laid during a sabbatical spent at the Harvard Business School and at Boston College's School of Management. My thanks to the academic and administrative staffs of these institutions and of Bar-Ilan's Department of Sociology and Anthropology for providing me with congenial and stimulating work environments. In particular my deep thanks to Arthur Turner, who sponsored my visit to Harvard, provided valuable feedback on my work, and contributed greatly to my understanding of the effect of interpersonal processes on consulting. Thomas Backer, Jean Bartunek, Leonard Bickman, Jo-Ann Harrison, Dafna Izraeli, Debra Rog, and an anonymous reader read the manuscript of the first edition and made invaluable suggestions for its improvement. Peter Bamberger, Jean Bartunek, Jo-Ann Harrison, Dafna Izraeli, Bruce Phillips, and Aryeh Shirom provided helpful reactions to papers that preceded this revised edition and parts of the revised manuscript. I also wish to acknowledge my all-too-brief association with the late Ed Huse and the advice and encouragement of Jim Bowditch, Judy Gordon, Dal Fisher, Jack Lewis, Bill Torbert, and other colleagues at Boston College and Bar-Ilan. Thanks also to Hadassah Rahab, Kumiko DiSalva, Clare White-Sullivan, and Yoshio Saito for assistance on the first edition of the book.

Finally, I want to express my deepest appreciation to my wife, Jo-Ann, and my son, Nathan, for their support and encouragement throughout this project. This book is dedicated to them, my father, my brother, and the memories of my mother, Joan Kant Harrison, and my mother-in-law, Ruth Bitensky Schonfeld.

MICHAEL I. HARRISON

1

Diagnosis: Approaches and Methods

This chapter examines the main features of diagnosis and its uses in behavioral science consultations that are aimed at organizational improvement and change. Three critical facets of diagnosis are introduced: (1) *process*—working with members of an organization to plan and administer a diagnostic study and providing feedback on the findings; (2) *interpretation*—using behavioral science models to frame issues for study, to identify conditions underlying the problems presented by members, and to analyze diagnostic findings; (3) *methods*—techniques for collecting and summarizing diagnostic data.

Organizational diagnosis is the process of using conceptual models and methods from the behavioral sciences to assess an organization's current state and find ways to solve specific problems or increase its effectiveness.[1] Diagnosis guides the development of proposals for organizational change and improvement by consultants and their clients. Managers can also improve their capacity for decision making and problem solving by applying the diagnostic approach without the aid of consultants (Glueck, 1982; Gordon, 1991). Here are two examples of the use of diagnosis in consulting projects in which I took part.[2]

Case 1

A new management team sought to transform a large transport cooperative that was handicapped by a tradition of paternalistic management, political infighting, and deal making. The team wanted to run the firm according to principles of business management rather than political bargaining. The team asked a private behavioral science consulting firm for help in planning and implementing this transformation. Overburdened with minor problems originating in the local branches, management sought advice on ways to improve

1. The term *behavioral science* refers to the social and behavioral sciences.

2. Unless otherwise noted all of the cases in this book are based on my own experience or that of my colleagues.

decision making and to enhance coordination of field operations. Members of the consulting firm interviewed managers in the field and at headquarters, culled company records for evidence of communication and decision-making processes, and observed local- and national-level meetings. The consultants recommended structural and administrative reforms that would reduce pressure on top management and would fit the firm's overall reorganization program.

Case 2

In cooperation with the chief personnel officer, a human resources unit within the armed forces prepared a survey of organizational climate and leadership in field units. Repeat applications of the survey allowed for comparisons within units over time as well as for comparisons between functionally similar units at the same point in time. Members of the human resources unit located in the field provided periodic feedback to commanding officers as a stimulus to improving leadership and administrative practices.

In both of these cases, clients requested advice from consultants. The main clients for a diagnosis are the people who bear most of the responsibility for deciding what actions, if any, to take in light of the diagnostic findings and for planning and implementing these actions. These people are usually the ones who originally solicited and sponsored the study. Clients are often top administrators, as in the two cases presented above. But union-management teams (e.g., Shirom, 1983), mid-level managers, entire working groups, owners, and supervisory agencies may also act as clients. In some change projects, special steering committees are set up parallel to, but outside of, the operating hierarchy of the organization. These steering groups define project goals, plan interventions, and supervise project implementation (Rubenstein & Woodman, 1984; Stein & Kanter, 1980).

Clients play a critical role in defining the consultation's goals (see chapter 6) and in shaping relations between the consultants and the organization. In the cases described above, the clients turned to consultants trained in the behavioral sciences because the clients assumed that their organization's problems and challenges related to people, groups, and organizational arrangements rather than involving mainly business or technical issues. Clients often refer initially to problems such as:

- Low productivity, high costs, and other signs of inefficiency.

- Difficulty starting or completing complex projects (e.g., drive to enhance customer service, implementing new technologies).
- Declining demand for products or services, client/customer dissatisfaction, falling revenues, criticism by external stakeholders.
- Problems in making major transitions (e.g., from family to professionally managed firm, mergers, changes of ownership or management).
- Employee turnover, stress, and health problems, low morale; poor work quality, neglect of equipment.
- Extreme conflicts and tensions, repeated misunderstandings and communication failures.
- Problems in managing a multicultural workforce or operating in an unfamiliar region or nation.
- Disruptions of work flows between groups, tasks falling between the cracks, frequent delays and crises; red tape, needless duplication of functions.
- Missed opportunities (e.g., lack of innovation and new ideas; competitors enter new areas faster).
- External threats and challenges (e.g., changes in government regulations or market conditions).

In other cases, clients may request an assessment of how well the organization functions in a specific areas such as staff development (e.g., Case 7, chapter 3). Or they may seek advice on how to improve operations in areas such as quality, customer service, productivity, or creativity and innovativeness. Such concerns have led to consultations and change projects in public-sector organizations such as schools, hospitals, city governments, and the military; private firms in areas such as manufacturing, banking, and retailing; voluntary groups including charities and religious groups; and cooperative businesses and communities.

The behavioral science *consultants* (or *practitioners*) to whom clients turn are specialists in organization development, applied research, human resources management, or related fields. These practitioners provide advice and other services to members of the organization (Turner, 1982). When clients undertake complex organizational changes, they often employ consultants from a range of fields, including industrial engineering, marketing, and business strategy (Nees & Greiner, 1985). Consultants to a single client organization may work independently or in coordination with one another, in keeping with client preferences and the nature of the project.

Besides being skilled at investigating and analyzing organizations, many behavioral science consultants are experienced in giving feedback and working with groups. The consultants can be located within the human resources unit within large corporations (McMahan & Woodman, 1992) or public-sector organizations (e.g., Case 2) or may be hired from the outside on a contractual basis (e.g., Case 1). External consultants are usually members of management consulting firms or are university faculty members specializing in organizational research and consulting. The scope of the project determines whether consultants work alone or in teams.

In the cases described above, the consultants conducted a diagnosis to understand the nature and causes of the problems or challenges initially presented by clients, to identify additional organizational problems and opportunities, to discover ways to solve these problems, and to improve organizational *effectiveness.* During diagnosis they compared the *current state* of the client organization to a *preferred state* (e.g., improved coordination of field operations in Case 1, improved relations between officers and subordinates in Case 2) and assessed effectiveness in terms of a standard (e.g., appropriate decision-making procedures; ratings of officers in comparable units). Moreover, each diagnostic study involved a search for ways to narrow the gap between the current and the desired state of affairs.

In light of the diagnostic findings, consultants often point to the need to change one or more key features of the organization. These include managerial goals or strategies (e.g., to appeal to a different clientele or market segment); members' skills, knowledge, and attitudes (e.g., the ability to work with people from different cultures); interpersonal and intergroup processes (e.g., leadership patterns), organizational structures (e.g., division into departments, links to other organizations); and work technologies. Moreover, consultants may recommend a wide range of interventions that management or other clients can undertake to bring about the desired improvements. Clients sometimes ask the practitioners who conducted the diagnosis or other consultants to help them implement these steps toward improvement.

USES OF DIAGNOSIS

Diagnosis can contribute to many types of consultations for organizational change. Let us compare its use in different types of change projects.

Independent Diagnostic Studies

Diagnosis can take the form of an independent consulting project, in which practitioners contract with clients about the nature of the study, design it, gather and analyze the data, and provide written and oral feedback on their findings and recommendations. In these projects formal relations between clients and consultants end with the delivery of the diagnostic report. Consultants and clients often prefer this approach for highly focused studies, in which management is assumed to have the capability to implement the diagnostic recommendations.

Independent diagnostic studies can also facilitate managerial efforts to bring about complex, far-reaching *organizational transformations* (Bartunek & Louis, 1988; Kilmann, Covin, et al., 1988) such as basic changes in the organization's goals, strategies, and culture. Transformations usually require members of the organization to bend or break out of accepted ways of thinking and acting and to develop new frames for understanding and evaluating their work (Bartunek & Moch, 1987; Nadler, 1988). Such changes usually evolve over a period of several years under the leadership of top management (Tichy & DeVanna, 1986). Efforts to achieve transformations often occur after major shifts in power alignments within and outside of the organization or after organizations have undergone crises that threaten their survival. To accomplish such fundamental changes, management may draw on the advice of consultants with expertise in many different areas.

Diagnostic studies can help management assess the need for transformation, determine whether the organization has the capacity to accomplish such major changes, discover ways to enhance this capacity, choose ways to intervene in the organization to bring about change, and monitor the effects of these interventions. Sometimes behavioral scientists intervene directly in organizations undergoing transformation by explaining change programs to members, training them in needed skills (e.g., teamwork, quality assessment), and helping management revise its plans and goals in the light of internal and external developments during the transformation period. The Contemporary Health Facilities project described below (Case 5) illustrates an independent diagnostic study of the need and prospects for organizational transformation.

Diagnosis in Program Assessment and Design

When clients ask experts to provide advice about a specific set of administrative activities (such as employee safety programs) or to design specific programs for an organization, the consultants often begin by conducting a diagnosis of relevant features of the current state of the organization. In these projects, diagnosis provides the data needed to guide recommendations for improving current programs or designing new ones. Case 7 (chapter 3), for example, describes how practitioners might assess the degree to which management training programs in a multinational firm build the skills needed for managing operations on a worldwide basis. An assessment study such as this could serve as the basis for developing recommendations for redesigning the firm's management training activities to meet the challenges posed by globalization.

Diagnosis as a Stage in Organization Development

Diagnosis also plays a crucial role in organization development projects—a term that includes action research and planned change (Cummings & Huse, 1989).

Organization Development Stages

Extended organization development projects go through a series of stages (Kolb & Frohman, 1970). Projects usually begin with a *scouting stage,* in which clients and consultants get to know one another and consultants gain their first impressions of the client organization. After the consultant and clients clarify their expectations for the consultation and formalize them in a *contract,* the consultant conducts a *diagnosis* of the current state of the organization and provides *feedback to clients* on the findings. Thereafter consultants and clients work together to *define objectives* for the change project and *plan interventions* that will promote desired changes. During the *action stage,* the consultants guide or actually conduct these interventions, sometimes gathering additional diagnostic data and providing additional feedback. Thereafter, clients and consultants evaluate the results of the project. In practice, consultation in organization development often shifts back and forth between these stages, rather than following them sequentially (e.g., Case 4).

Behavioral science consultants have developed a wide range of intervention techniques to facilitate organizational change (Bennis, Benne, & Chin, 1985; Burke, 1982; Cummings & Huse, 1989; Porras & Robertson, 1987; Tichy, 1983). Here, grouped by the major target, are interventions sometimes conducted or facilitated by behavioral scientists:

Members: changing or selecting for skills, attitudes, and values through training programs and courses; recruitment, selection, counseling, and placement; stress management and health-maintenance programs.

Behavior and processes: changing interaction processes, such as decision making, leadership, and communication through training, team building, process consultation, third-party intervention for conflict resolution; feedback of survey data for self-diagnosis and action planning.

Organizational structures and technologies: redesigning jobs, administrative procedures, reward mechanisms, the division of labor, coordinating mechanisms, work procedures (e.g., replacing assembly line with work teams).

Organizational goals, strategies, and cultures: promoting goal clarification and strategy formulation through workshops and exercises; facilitating cooperative ties between organizations, examining and changing corporate cultures (values, norms, beliefs).

Consultants rely on several sources of knowledge as they decide which intervention techniques are likely to produce the desired results. These sources include evidence gathered during diagnosis, the consultants' experience, books and papers by practitioners, and a small but growing body of research (Bullock & Tubbs, 1987; Porras & Robertson, 1992; Porras & Silver, 1992).

Consultants can engage in diagnostic activities during many phases of a consultation. During scouting, consultants may unobtrusively observe interactions between clients and other members of the organization to get a feel for interpersonal processes and power relations. At the same time, consultants may also conduct interviews or discussions with important members to become familiar with the organization and to assess the members' attitudes toward the proposed consulting project. Consultants will also read available documents on the organization's history, goals, and current operations.

Based on this information, consultants usually make a *preliminary diagnosis* of the organization's needs and strengths and its capacity for improvement and change. This preliminary diagnosis can determine the subsequent development of the project. The experienced practitioner seeks to determine as early as possible whether members of an organization are likely to cooperate with a more formal diagnostic study and how willing and able they are to reach decisions and act in response to feedback. As consultants and clients discuss these preliminary assessments, they redefine their expectations for the consultation. This process increases the chances that the consultation will benefit the clients and helps both parties avoid entering a relationship that will become an exercise in frustration.

Diagnosis itself can be a form of intervention, since it interrupts organizational routines, may affect members' expectations concerning change, and may influence how they think about themselves and their organization (Argyris, 1970). In *process consultation* (Schein, 1969), for example, the practitioner provides diagnostic feedback on group processes to heighten awareness of these processes and thereby help participants improve them. Similarly, practitioners sometimes conduct *diagnostic workshops* for management teams or steering committees responsible for change projects. The workshops are intended to promote teamwork and facilitate planning and decision making. During the workshops, the consultants may lead participants to examine their organization's culture (Lundberg, 1990), clarify their goals and strategies (Jayaram, 1976; chapter 5), or choose and implement appropriate organization designs (Stebbins & Shani, 1989).

Moving Beyond Traditional Organization Development

Although organizational diagnosis has strong roots in the organization development tradition, practitioners of diagnosis need to move beyond that tradition to develop a broader and more flexible approach to diagnosis and consulting. Until recently most organization development envisioned a broad role for consultants in helping organizations plan and introduce change. These consultants assumed that organizations are most effective when they reduce power differences, foster open communication, encourage cooperation and solidarity, and adopt policies that enhance the potential of employees (Strauss, 1976). To promote development toward this ideal type of structure and culture, organization development consultants often used experiential small group training (e.g., Dyer, 1977), feedback on interpersonal processes (Schein, 1969), and participative decision making (French & Bell, 1984). During the 1980s, management best-sellers such as *In Search of Excellence* (Peters & Waterman, 1982) and *Theory Z* (Ouchi, 1981) spurred a new wave of enthusiasm for organization development values such as open communication, employee participation in decision making, and the importance of a strong, cohesive organizational culture.

Today, many researchers and behavioral science consultants acknowledge that the traditional organization development model was based on a very narrow view of organizational effectiveness (see chapter 2). Moreover, the training and small-group interventions favored by organization development practitioners often failed to grapple with the realities of organizational politics and culture. For these reasons traditional organization development techniques do not seem to work well in organizations that emphasize status and authority differences (Bartunek & Moch, 1987; Passmore, Petee, & Bastian, 1986; Reason, 1984) or in nations that do not share the values underlying organization development (e.g., Faucheux, Amando, & Laurent, 1982; Jaeger, 1986; Kiggundu, 1986). Even where they are appropriate, traditional organization development interventions usually yield minor, incremental improvements in organizational functioning, as opposed to the radical transformations needed for recovery from crises and decline (Dunphy & Stace, 1988).

Spurred by such findings, this book adopts an approach to organizational change and effectiveness that is gradually supplanting the views of traditional organization development. Here are four major features of this new approach: First, change and effectiveness are very much affected by macro-organizational forces—organizational structure, technology, environmental relations, strategy, and organizational culture (e.g., Daft, 1992). Second, power alignments and political bargaining in and around organizations play a crucial role in organizational consultation and planned change (Greiner & Schein, 1988; Harrison, 1991; Kakabadse & Parker, 1984). Third, managerial and consultant roles in planned change necessarily vary across the organizational life cycle and are shaped by the organization's overall state of growth, stability, decline, or crisis (Adizes, 1988; Harrison, 1991; Mintzberg, 1984). Fourth, consultants can facilitate major organizational changes and transformations, but managers typically drive them (Beer & Walton, 1987; Kilmann et al., 1988; Tichy & DeVanna, 1986). To contribute to organizational change, diagnosis needs to draw on this revised approach and to reflect the broad range of recent organizational research and consulting practice.

Self-Diagnosis

Members of an organization can conduct a self-diagnosis without the aid of a professional consultant if they are open to self-analysis and criticism and if some members have the skills needed for the gathering and interpretation of information. Here is an example of a modest self-diagnosis (Austin, 1982, p. 20):

Case 3

The executive director of a multiservice youth agency appointed a program-review committee to make a general evaluation of the services provided by the agency and make recommendations for improving its effectiveness. The committee included clinical case workers, supervisors, administrators, and several members of the

> agency's governing board. The director of the agency, who had technical knowledge to conduct such a study, served as an advisor to the committee. She asked the committee members to look first at the agency's intake service, because it was central to the operations of the entire agency and suffered from high turnover among its paid staff. Besides examining intake operations, the committee members decided to investigate whether clients were getting appropriate services. They interviewed both the paid and the volunteer intake staff and surveyed clients over a 3-month period. Their main finding was that there were substantial delays in client referral to counseling. They traced these delays to the difficulties that the half-time coordinator of intake faced in handling the large staff, many of whom were volunteers, and to the heavy burden of record keeping that fell on the intake workers. This paperwork was required by funding agencies but did not contribute directly to providing services to clients. To increase the satisfaction of the intake staff and thereby reduce turnover, the committee recommended that the coordinator's position be made full time and that the paperwork at intake be reduced. The executive director accepted the first recommendation and asked for further study of how to streamline the record-keeping process and reduce paperwork.

As this case suggests, during self-diagnosis, members of the organization temporarily take on some of the tasks that would otherwise be the responsibility of a professional consultant. Many of the diagnostic models and research techniques described in this book and in other guides to diagnosis (e.g., Lauffer, 1982, 1984; Manzini, 1988; Weisbord, 1978) could contribute to such self-studies. People who want to conduct a self-diagnosis or act as consultants should be skilled at handling the interpersonal relations that develop during a study, at giving feedback to groups and individuals, and at gathering and analyzing diagnostic data.

Comparisons to Other Types of Organizational Research

Another way of understanding diagnosis is to contrast it to other forms of organizational research. As defined here, diagnosis does not include investigations of programs by commissions of inquiry or governmental agencies. These investigations do not create client-consultant relations of the sort described above and do not rely heavily on behavioral science methods and models. Nor does diagnosis refer to the many forms of applied research (Freeman, Dynes, Rossi, & Whyte, 1983; Majchrzak, 1984), which may help decision makers formulate policies and allocate funds. These studies usually have a narrower research focus than diagnosis. For example, applied research might seek to isolate the forces affecting a particular organizational process, such as grievance resolution. Or they may seek to explain the variance in an outcome of concerns such as alcohol abuse or work accidents.

Diagnosis has more in common with evaluation research (Rossi & Freeman, 1993), in which behavioral science research contributes to the planning, monitoring, and assessment of the costs and impacts of social programs in areas such as health, education, and welfare (e.g., the impact of reading readiness program on preschoolers). Like diagnosis, evaluation is practically oriented and may focus on effectiveness. But diagnostic studies often examine a broader spectrum of indicators of organizational effectiveness than do *summative evaluations,* which assess program impacts or program efficiency. Diagnostic studies also differ from most *formative evaluations,* which monitor program implementation. Most diagnostic studies examine a broad range of organizational features, whereas formative evaluations usually concentrate on the extent to which a project was conducted according to plan. An additional difference is that diagnoses are often conducted on much more restricted budgets, within shorter time frames, and must rely on less extensive forms of data gathering and analysis.

Diagnosis differs substantially from nonapplied, academic research on organizations in its emphasis on obtaining results that will be immediately useful to members of a client organization (Block, 1981, p. 142). Unlike academic researchers, practitioners of diagnosis:

- Concentrate on finding readily changeable factors that affect an organizational problem or condition, even if these factors do not explain most of the variance and are not the most important or interesting from a researcher's point of view.
- May encourage the members of the organization under study to become involved in the research.
- May use less complex research designs and methods (e.g., simpler sampling procedures, a few open-ended observational categories instead of many precoded ones, fewer control variables) to conform to practical constraints (time, resources, data availability) and client preferences.
- Need to rely more on hunches, experience, and intuition as well as on scientific methods when gathering and analyzing data and formulating conclusions and recommendations.

- Cannot remain neutral about the impact of their study on the organization and the needs and concerns of members of the organization.

THREE FACETS OF DIAGNOSIS

Key Success Factors in Diagnosis

Unlike conventional research, successful diagnosis requires more than the skillful gathering and analysis of data. A diagnostic study can only succeed if it provides its clients with data, interpretations, and recommendations that are both valid and useful (see Judd, Smith, & Kidder, 1991; Tyson, Ackerman, Domsch, & Joynt, 1988, on validity; Lawler, Nadler, & Cammann, 1980, pp. 11-18; and Turner, 1982, on evaluative criteria). To meet these standards the diagnostic practitioner must fill the requirements of three key facets of diagnosis—*process, interpretation,* and *methods*—and must create good matches among these three facets.

Process

The texture of client-consultant relations poses clear requirements for successful diagnosis: To provide genuinely useful findings and recommendations, consultants need to create and maintain cooperative, constructive relations with clients. Moreover, to insure that their study yields valid and useful results, practitioners of diagnosis must successfully negotiate their relations with other members of the focal organization.

Phases in Diagnosis

Diagnostic studies typically include several distinct phases (Nadler, 1977). As the following description shows, the diagnostic tasks, models, and methods shift within and between phases, as do relations between consultants, clients, and other members of the client organization:

Scouting: Clients and consultants explore expectations for the study; client presents problems, challenges; consultant assesses likelihood of cooperation with various types of research, probable receptiveness to feedback and makes a preliminary reconnaissance of organizational problems and strengths.

Contracting: Consultants and clients negotiate and agree on the nature of the diagnosis and client-consultant relations.

Study design: Methods, measurement procedures, sampling, analysis, and administrative procedures are planned.

Data gathering: Data are gathered through interviews, observations, questionnaires, analysis of secondary data, group discussions, and workshops.

Analysis: The data are organized and summarized. Consultants (and sometimes clients) interpret them and prepare for feedback.

Feedback: Consultants present findings to clients and other members of the client organization. Feedback may include explicit recommendations or more general findings to stimulate discussion, decision making, and action planning.

As Case 4 suggests, these phases can overlap in practice and their sequence may vary:

Case 4

The owner and president of 21C, a small high-technology firm, asked a private consultant to examine ways to improve efficiency and morale in the firm. They agreed that staff from the consulting firm would conduct a set of in-depth interviews with divisional managers and a sample of other employees. The first interviews with the three division heads and the assistant director suggested that their frustrations and poor morale stemmed from the firm's lack of growth and the president's failure to include the managers in decision making and strategy formulation. In light of these findings the consultant returned to the president, discussed the results of the interviews and suggested refocusing the diagnosis on the relations between the managers and the president and on planning and strategy formulation within the firm.

In the 21 C project, analysis and feedback began before the data gathering phase was completed. During data gathering the diagnosis shifted back into the contracting phase when the consultant sought approval to redefine the diagnostic problem and change the research design.

Key Process Issues

The relations that develop between practitioners and members of a client organization can greatly affect the outcomes of an organizational diagnosis, just as they affect other aspects of consulting (Turner, 1982;

Block, 1981). Although clients and practitioners should try to define their expectations early in the project, they will often need to redefine their relations during the course of the diagnosis to deal with issues that were neglected during initial contracting or arose subsequently.[3] To manage the consulting relation successfully, practitioners need to handle the following key process issues (Nadler, 1977; Van de Ven & Ferry, 1980, pp. 22-51) in ways that promote cooperation between themselves and members of the client organization and promote the objectives of the consultation:

Purpose: What are the goals of the study, how are they defined, and how can the outcomes of the study be evaluated? What issues, challenges, and problems are to be studied?

Design: How will the study design and methods affect members of the organization (organizational features to be studied, units and individuals included in the data gathering, and types of data-collection techniques)?

Support and cooperation: Who sponsors and supports the study and what resources will the client organization contribute? What are the attitudes of other members of the organization and of external stakeholders toward the study?

Participation: What role will members of the organization play in planning the study, gathering, interpreting, and reacting to the data?

Feedback: When, how, and in what format will feedback be given? Who will receive feedback on the study and what uses will they make of the data?

Participation: Consultant Versus Client-Centered Diagnosis

As these questions suggest, clients and consultants must make difficult and consequential decisions concerning participation in the study by members of the focal organization. Self-contained diagnostic studies are usually *consultant-centered,* since the consultant accepts sole or primary responsibility for conducting all phases of the diagnosis. Once the clients approve the proposed study, they and other members of the organization may not take an active role in it until they receive feedback on the findings. Practitioners often prefer this type of diagnosis because it seems simpler and more suitable to objective, rigorous research. Clients too often prefer to limit their investment in diagnosis and to wait for the results of the study before committing themselves to additional interventions.

An all-too-frequent result of this separation of diagnosis from action is that clients take no action on the consultant's recommendations

3. Suggestions that are addressed to consultants (or practitioners) are intended for would-be and beginning practitioners as well as for more experienced ones.

because they see them as irrelevant or unworkable (Block, 1981; Turner, 1982). Skillful consultants may partially overcome this problem by meeting periodically with clients to discuss findings and interpretations and by asking clients to draw conclusions from these results. In this fashion, consultants increase the chances that their findings will reflect the experiences and perceptions of key clients and will therefore be believable to clients. Moreover, periodic discussions of the study may encourage clients to feel more responsibility for diagnostic findings and recommendations.

In contrast to consultant-centered studies, diagnosis within organization development projects is often highly *client-centered,* in the sense of involving clients or members appointed by them in as many phases of diagnosis as is feasible (Turner, 1982; Lawler & Drexler, 1980). This approach encourages members of the client organization to contribute their insights and expertise as they share in data gathering and analysis. Besides enhancing the credibility and salience of diagnostic findings, participation in diagnosis may help members develop the capacity to assess their own operations. This capacity for routine self-assessment can help members develop the ability to cope continually with social, technological, and economic changes (Cummings & Huse, 1989, pp. 439-443; Nadler, Mirvis, & Cammann, 1976; Torbert, 1981; Wildavsky, 1972).

Despite these advantages, client-centered diagnosis has serious limitations and drawbacks. First, it is only likely to have the sought-for effects when the culture of the client organization supports open communication and the honest confrontation of organizational and individual limitations. Second, active participation in diagnosis by members of the client organization may raise questions about the study's objectivity and may lead people to fear that their responses or observed behavior will not remain confidential. Third, client-centered diagnosis may actually endanger the prospects for organizational change by giving opponents of change added opportunities to delay or divert steps toward change. This risk is greatest when developments such as decline or reorganization threaten the survival, prestige, or power of some members of the organization.

Interpretation

The success of a diagnosis depends greatly on the ways that practitioners handle the interpretive tasks of defining diagnostic problems, choosing topics for study, analyzing results, and preparing recommendations. Findings and models from the social and behavioral sciences can provide guides to gathering and interpreting diagnostic findings (Tichy, 1983). These models specify key concepts and variables and point to important relations among them. Unlike formal theories (Bacharach, 1989), models do not usually specify these relations precisely. Moreover, most social science models select a few aspects of organizational life while neglecting others (Morgan, 1986).

To provide useful findings and recommendations, practitioners must assure that their results are important and relevant to clients. Thus during diagnosis practitioners must learn what organizational outcomes clients value and find ways to help them achieve these particular outcomes. Practitioners can then introduce additional criteria for assessing the effectiveness of the organization that clients had ignored or played down. For example, diagnosis might help clients see that management's emphasis on short-term achievements leads employees to ignore activities that could contribute to valuable results in the long run (e.g., Case 8 in chapter 4).

As this example suggests, practitioners can often make their greatest contribution to organizational improvement by reinterpreting the problems and issues presented by clients. Besides contributing additional effectiveness criteria, reinterpretation can help consultants and clients understand and attack causes of problems, rather than symptoms. Moreover, by identifying underlying organizational features and conditions, practitioners can point to links between conditions that members previously viewed as unrelated. Redefining the problems and challenges facing a unit can also help clients build consensus and support for needed changes. For example, feedback of data showing that low quality and noncompetitive labor costs endanger an organization's survival can help management and labor discover their common interest in finding ways to solve these problems.

Here is a summary of a diagnostic project that I conducted that illustrates how the consultant may define more broadly the problem presented by the client. The case also illustrates the interplay among diagnostic processes, interpretations, and methods. Furthermore, the case shows how practitioners and clients negotiate their relations and how there can be more than one client for a diagnosis.

Case 5

The head of training of a national health care system received a request from the director of one of its member organizations—here called Contemporary Health Facilities (CHF)—for an ambitious program that would train its employees to undertake a major organizational transformation. The transformation proposed by the director would radically redefine the goals and mission of CHF. Moreover, it would alter patient characteristics, personnel, the size and structure of CHF, and its relations with other health-care organizations. The director was worried that CHF's nursing staff and administrative employees would oppose the far-reaching changes he envisioned for CHF.

Not convinced that the training program was justified, the head of training reached an agreement with CHF's director to ask an independent practitioner to assess the situation. After meetings between the practitioner, the head of training, and the top administrators at CHF, all parties agreed to broaden the study goals to include assessment of the feasibility of the planned transformation and the staff's readiness for the change. Training was to be considered as only one of the possible steps that might facilitate the change.

Over a 3-week period the practitioner conducted in-depth interviews with CHF's three top administrators and seven staff members in positions of authority. In addition, he conducted group interviews with 12 lower-level staff members, made site visits, and examined data on CHF's personnel, patient characteristics, and administration. The practitioner interpreted and presented these data within the context of a guiding model (derived in part from Tichy, 1983) of the preconditions for strategic organizational change. The major finding was that the transformation was both desirable and feasible, although accomplishing it would be risky and difficult. The report to the CHF administration and the director of training conveyed these conclusions and some of the findings on which they were based. Moreover, it recommended steps that the director of CHF should take to overcome opposition and build support for the proposed transformation of CHF and ways of implementing the transformation. The report also recommended ways to improve organizational climate, enhance staffing procedures, and improve other aspects of organizational effectiveness with or without implementing the program to transform CHF.

The director of training originally phrased the diagnostic problem in terms of assessing the need for the training program requested by CHF's director. The practitioner helped reframe this issue by dividing it into two more basic issues: assessing the feasibility of accomplishing the organizational transformation envisioned by the director and discovering steps that the administration could take to facilitate the transformation. This redefinition of the diagnostic problem thus included an image of the organization's desired state that fit both client expectations and social science knowledge about organizational effectiveness. Moreover, this reformulation helped specify the issues that should be studied in depth and suggested ways that the clients could deal with the problem that initially concerned them. In formulating their recommendations the consultant took into account which possible solutions to problems were more likely to be accepted and could be successfully implemented by the clients (see chapter 2).

Interpretive Questions

The following set of questions that consultants can ask themselves (based partly on Beckhard, 1969, p. 46, and Block, 1981, p. 143) highlights key issues. The term *problem* refers here to cover any kind of gap between actual and ideal conditions, including challenges to enter new fields and raise performance standards.

1. *Interpreting the initial statement of the problem.* How does the client initially define the problems, needs, and challenges facing the organization or unit? How does the client view the desired state of the organization?
2. *Redefining the problem.* How can the problem be redefined to be investigated and have workable solutions developed? What assumptions about the preferred state of the organization and definitions of organizational effectiveness will be used in the diagnosis? How will solving the problem contribute to organizational effectiveness? What aspects of organizational life will be the focal points of the diagnosis?
3. *Understanding the current state.* What individuals, groups, and components of the organization are most affected by this redefined problem and most likely to be involved in or affected by its solution? What is their current state? How is the problem currently being dealt with? How do members of the relevant groups define the problem and suggest solving it? What organizational resources and strengths could contribute to solving the problem and improving effectiveness?
4. *Identifying the forces for and against change.* What internal and external groups and conditions create pressure for organizational change and what are the sources of resistance to it? How ready and capable of changing are the people and groups who are most affected by the problem and its possible solutions? Do they have common interests or needs that could become a basis for working together to solve the problem?

5. *Developing workable solutions.* Which behavior patterns and organizational arrangements, if any, can be most easily changed to solve problems and improve effectiveness? What interventions are most likely to produce these desired outcomes?

In some diagnoses, clients and other members of the focal organization take most of the responsibility for the fourth and fifth tasks. Even in such cases, however, the analysis and feedback reflect practitioners' assumptions about how to improve the organization.

Level of Analysis

A major interpretive issue facing consultants concerns the level of analysis at which they will examine a problem and suggest dealing with it. Questions about people's attitudes, motivations, and work behavior focus on the *individual level.* Those dealing with face-to-face relations are at the *interpersonal level.* At the *group level* are questions about the performance and practices of departments or work units, such as those raised in Case 3. Then come questions at the *divisional level* about the management of major subunits (divisions, branches, factories) within large organizations and about relations among units within divisions. Some investigations, like the study of CHF, examine the *organization* as a whole and its relations to its environment. Finally, in rare cases, diagnosis examines a set of interacting organizations or an entire *sector* or *industry,* such as the health-care sector (Shirom, 1993b).

Many important phenomena show up at more than one level of analysis. In a manufacturing division, for example, the main technology (work tools and techniques) might be computer-aided manufacturing, which uses robots and flexible manufacturing systems (Sussman, 1990). At the group level, each work group would have its own techniques and equipment for monitoring the highly automated operations. At the individual level are specific equipment and control procedures at each work station. Certain other phenomena can best be observed at one particular level. For instance, the speed with which the firm decides to make new products, develops them, and brings them to market can best be examined at the level of the total organization.

The choice of levels of analysis in diagnosis should reflect the nature of the problem, the goals of the diagnosis, and the organizational location of the clients. To facilitate the diagnosis and increase the chances that clients will implement recommendations, practitioners should concentrate on organizational features over which their clients have considerable control. Changes in the departmental structure of an entire division, for example, can occur only with the support of top management. Furthermore, consultants should focus their diagnoses on levels at which interventions are most likely to lead to organizational improvement. For example, if managers asked for a diagnosis of problems related to employee performance, consultants would examine the rules and procedures for monitoring, controlling, and rewarding performance, if these design tools could be readily changed by managerial clients. Other influential factors, such as workers' informal relations and their work norms and values, might be more difficult to change.

By raising or lowering the level of analysis, consultants and clients can sometimes discover relations and possibilities for change that were not previously apparent. For instance, rather than concentrating exclusively on administrator-subordinate relations within an underproductive department in a public agency, consultants might look at the group's location within the work flow of the entire division. This shift in level of analysis might point to coordination problems within the division as a whole that must be solved before work-group productivity can be improved.

Scope

Practitioners must also decide on the scope of their study. An individual-level diagnosis of broad scope, for example, would try to take into account of the major factors related to the performance and feelings of the people within a focal unit (see chapter 3). In contrast, a more narrowly focused individual-level diagnosis within the same unit might look only at factors related to job satisfaction.

Models

Social science models can help practitioners decide what to study, choose measures of organizational effectiveness, and identify conditions that promote or block effectiveness. Practitioners of diagnosis can also obtain guidance from sets of models, theories, and empirical studies that serve as metaphors (Morgan, 1986) or frames (Bolman & Deal, 1991), in the sense that they lead us to look at distinctive organizational phenomena that might not be evident from some other perspective. For example, questions about the forces for and against change (see Interpretive Question 4) reflect a political frame of analysis (Lawler & Bacharach, 1983; Pfeffer, 1981b; chapters 3 and 6). In the CHF study, questions such as these were added to the issues raised by the open system model presented in chapter 2.

Although models and analytical frames based on current research can serve as guides to diagnosis, they cannot tell practitioners in advance exactly what to study, how to interpret diagnostic data, or what interventions will work best in a particular client organization. Research shows that managerial practices and organizational patterns that promote effectiveness in one type of organization (e.g., new family businesses) will not necessarily contribute to effectiveness in another organization faced with different conditions (e.g., mature, professionally managed firms). The chapters that follow note some of the important conditions or contingencies that help determine which facets of organizational effectiveness are most important and which managerial practices and organizational forms contribute most to effectiveness. But a book of this length cannot adequately discuss all of these contingencies (see Hall, 1987; Harrison & Phillips, 1991; Mintzberg, 1979; Pennings, 1992). For reference, here are some of the most important contingencies:

- Life-cycle stage—start-up, becoming a collectivity, formalizing rules, elaborating structure (Quinn & Cameron, 1983)
- Resource state—growing, stable, declining
- Organizational size and complexity
- Degree of bureaucratization
- Ownership
- Power alignments in and around the organization
- Overall purpose (e.g., profit or not-for-profit)
- Technology—uncertainty, complexity, routineness
- Workforce composition (e.g., occupational, educational, and skill levels)
- Sectoral or institutional setting (e.g., social welfare, military, manufacturing, banking)
- Strategy for coping with the environment (e.g., mass marketing or specialization)
- Environmental conditions—predictability, competitiveness; munificence, external dependencies
- Organizational culture
- Cultural context—national, regional, occupational, sectoral-institutional

Within the constraints imposed by such contingencies, individual managers and even rank and file employees can affect performance and influence the course of organizational change. People shape the organizations in which they work by interpreting organizational conditions, challenges, and opportunities and by acting in response to these understandings (Hrebiniak & Joyce, 1985; Pennings, 1992; Weick, 1979).

Since effectiveness can be defined in many ways, there is no single, ideal state for all organization (see chapter 2). Hence, consultants use many divergent models in diagnosis and recommend a wide range of intervention techniques for promoting effectiveness. So far, the virtues of most of these interventions have been demonstrated only in a preliminary fashion. Moreover, controversy prevails around the outcomes of change-oriented interventions and the best ways to assess these outcomes (Bullock & Svyantek, 1987; Bullock & Tubbs, 1987; Guzzo, Jackson, & Katzell, 1987). In view of this situation, the following chapters seek to convey the range of choices open to practitioners of diagnosis and their clients. Models that take account of important contingencies and allow for different definitions of effectiveness are preferred to those advocating one best way to achieve effectiveness (e.g., Likert, 1967; Peters & Waterman, 1982). Special emphasis is given to models that suggest how managers can negotiate external relations and redesign organizational structures and practices to fit the constraints within which they work.

Methods

The methods used to gather and analyze data can also determine the success of a diagnosis.

Choosing Methods

To provide valid results, practitioners should employ the most rigorous methods possible within the practical constraints imposed by the nature of the assignment. Rigorous methods (which need not be quantitative) follow accepted standards of scientific inquiry. They have a high probability of producing results that are valid (Judd et al., 1991) and could be replicated by other trained investigators. Nonrigorous approaches can yield valid results, but these cannot be externally evaluated or replicated. In assessing the validity of their diagnoses, practitioners need to be especially aware of the risk of false positive results that might lead them to recommend steps that are unjustified and even harmful to the client organization (Rossi & Whyte, 1983).

To achieve reliability (i.e., reproducibility) practitioners can turn to structured data-gathering and measurement techniques, such as fixed-choice questionnaires or observations using a standard coding scheme. Unfortunately, it is very hard to structure techniques for assessing many complex but important phenomena such as the degree to which managers accurately interpret environmental developments.

To produce valid and reliable results, investigators often must sort out conflicting opinions and perspectives about the organization to construct an independent assessment. The quest for an independent viewpoint and scientific rigor should not, however, prevent investigators from treating the plurality of interests and perspectives within a focal organization as a significant organizational feature in its own right (Hennestad, 1988; Ramirez & Bartunek, 1989).

Whatever techniques practitioners use in diagnosis, they should avoid methodological overkill when they need only a rough estimate of the extent of a particular phenomenon (Freeman & Rossi, 1984). In Case 4, for example, the investigators needed to determine whether division heads were frustrated and dissatisfied and if so, the sources of these feelings. But the practitioners did not need to specify the precise degree of managerial dissatisfaction, as they might have done in an academic research study.

Consultants need to consider the implications of their methods for the consulting process and the interpretive issues at hand as well as weighing strictly practical and methodological considerations. Thus consultants might prefer to use nonrigorous methods, such as discussions of organizational conditions in workshop settings, because these methods can enhance the commitment of participants to the diagnostic study and its findings. Or they might prefer observations to interviews, so as not to encourage people to expect that the consultation would address the many concerns that might be raised during interviews.

The methods chosen and the ways that data are presented to clients also need to fit the culture of the client organization. In a high technology firm, for example, people might regard qualitative research as too impressionistic and unscientific. On the other hand, members of a volunteer association might view the use of standardized questionnaires and quantitative analysis as too academic and impersonal.

Research Design

Three types of nonexperimental designs seem to be most useful in diagnosis. The first involves gathering data on important criteria that allow for comparisons between units or between entire organizations (e.g., Case 2). Comparisons may focus on criteria such as client satisfaction, the organizational climate (e.g., perceptions of peer and subordinate-supervisor relations, identification with unit and organizational goals), personnel turnover, costs, and sales. Sometimes practitioners can analyze available records or make repeated measurements to trace changes in key variables across time for each unit or for an entire set of related units.

The second design uses multivariate analysis of data to isolate the causes or predictors of variables linked to a particular organizational problem—such as work quality or employee turnover—or to some desirable outcome—such as product innovation or customer satisfaction. The third design uses qualitative field techniques to build a portrait of the operations of a small organization or subunit and to obtain in-depth data on subtle, hard-to-measure features that may be lost or distorted in close-ended inquiries. Among such features are members' perceptions, hidden assumptions, behind-the-scenes interactions, and work styles (see chapter 4). In such qualitative studies, investigators use the same kinds of data-gathering techniques and highly inductive forms of inference that are used in nonapplied qualitative studies (Lofland & Lofland, 1984; Miles & Huberman, 1984; A. Strauss, 1987; Van Maanen, 1979). However, qualitative diagnostic studies usually obtain less ethnographic detail than nonapplied qualitative research and use less rigorous forms of recording and analyzing field data.

Data Collection

Table 1.1 surveys and assesses data-collection techniques frequently used in diagnosis. Further details on these techniques appear in the chapters that follow, in standard texts on methods (e.g., Judd et al., 1991), in the references to the table, and in appendices A, B, and C.

No single method for gathering and analyzing data can suit every diagnostic problem and situation, just as there is no universal model for guiding diagnostic interpretations or one ideal procedure for managing the diagnostic process. By using several methods to gather and analyze their data, practitioners can compensate for many of the drawbacks associated with relying on a single method (Jick, 1979). They also need to choose methods that fit the diagnostic problems and contribute to cooperative, productive consulting relations.

PLAN OF THE BOOK

Chapter 2 shows practitioners how to use the open system model and a political model of organizations to get an overview of the functioning

Table 1.1
A Comparison of Methods for Gathering Diagnostic Data

Method	*Advantages*	*Disadvantages*
Questionnaires		
Self-administered schedules, fixed choices (chapter 3, Appendix B, this volume; Bowditch & Buono, 1989).	Easy to quantify and summarize results; quickest and cheapest way to gather new data rigorously; useful for large samples, repeated measures, comparisons between units or to norms; standardized instruments contain pretested items, reflect diagnostic models; good for studying attitudes and perceptions.	Hard to obtain data on structure, behavior; little information on contexts shaping behavior; not suited for subtle, sensitive issues; impersonal; risks: nonresponse, biased or invalid answers, overreliance on standardized measures and models.
Interviews		
Open-ended questions based on fixed schedule, interview guide, on-the-spot judgment (chapters 2, 3, 5, Appendix A, this volume; Greenbaum, 1988; McCracken, 1988; Schatzman & Strauss, 1973).	Readily cover many topics and features; can be modified before or during interview; can convey empathy, build trust; rich data; provide understanding of respondents' viewpoints and interpretations.	Expensive, sampling problems in large organizations; respondent and interviewer bias; noncomparable responses; hard to analyze and interpret responses to open-ended questions.
Observations		
Observations of people, work settings (chapters 2, 3, Appendix C, this volume; Lofland & Lofland, 1984; Schatzman & Strauss, 1973; Weick, 1985).	Behavioral data independent of self-descriptions, feelings, opinions; data on situational, contextual effects; rich data on hard-to-measure topics (e.g., actual practices, culture); data yield new insights, hypotheses.	Constraints on access (timing, distance, objections to intrusion by outsider); costly, time-consuming; observer bias, low interobserver reliability; may affect behavior of people observed; hard to analyze, interpret, report data; may seem unscientific.

(Continued)

of the client organization, choose topics for further diagnosis, assess organizational effectiveness, and decide what steps will help clients solve problems and enhance effectiveness. Chapters 3 through 5 explain how to diagnose individual and group behavior and organization-wide conditions. Special emphasis is placed on understanding power relations and other

Table 1.1
Continued

Method	*Advantages*	*Disadvantages*
Analyzing Available Records and Data		
Use of documents, reports, files, statistical records, unobtrusive measures (chapters 2, 5, this volume; Kinnear & Taylor, 1987, pp. 152-163, 177-188; Newson-Smith, 1986; Webb, Campbell, Schwartz, et al., 1966).	Nonreactive; often quantifiable; repeated measures show change; members of organization can help analyze data; credibility of familiar measures (e.g., customer complaints); often cheaper and faster than gathering new data; independent sources; data on total organization, environment.	Access, retrieval, analysis problems can raise costs and time requirements; validity, credibility of sources and measures can be low; need to analyze data in context; limited data on many topics.
Workshops, Group Discussions		
Discussions on group processes, culture, environmental challenges, strategy; directed by consultant or manager; simulations, exercises (chapter 5, this volume; Schein, 1969; Pfeiffer, 1993)	Useful data on complex, subtle processes; interactions can stimulate thinking, teamwork, planning; data available for immediate analysis and feedback; involvement of members in diagnosis; self-diagnosis possible; consultant can convey empathy, build trust.	Biases due to group processes, history, leaders' influence (e.g., stifle unpopular views); requires high levels of trust and cooperation within group; impressionistic, not rigorous, may yield superficial, biased results.

Derived in part from Bowditch & Buono (1989, pp. 32 -33), Nadler (1977, p. 119), Sutherland (1978, p. 163).

actual practices and on assessing an organization's ability to adjust to external constraints and take advantage of new developments in its environment. Exercises for students and practitioners-in-training appear at the end of chapters 1 through 5. Chapter 6 treats ethical and professional dilemmas confronting practitioners. The appendices give more details on diagnostic instruments and suggest how readers can develop their diagnostic and consulting skills. The summaries at the beginning of each chapter provide a more detailed view of the book's contents.

EXERCISE

You will probably find it easier and more satisfying to base all of the exercises in this book on the same organization. In addition to organizations where you work or where you know someone who can help you get access to information and people, consider the possibility of studying some part of the university, such as the housing office or the student union, or one of the many voluntary organizations found on campus and in the community. Once you have located an organization or unit (e.g., department, branch), discuss the possibility of studying it with a person who could give you permission to do so and could help you learn about the organization. Explain that you want to do several exercises designed to help you learn how behavioral science consultants and researchers can help organizations deal with issues and challenges confronting them and contribute to organizational effectiveness. Promise not to identify the organization and explain that your reports will be read only by your instructor.

If your contact expresses interest in becoming a client—in the sense of wanting to get feedback from your project—explain that you will be glad to provide oral feedback to the contact person only, provided that the anonymity of the people studied can be preserved. During these discussions try to learn as much about your contact person's job, his or her view of organizational affairs, degree of interest in your project, and how much help you can expect from this person. If possible, ask your contact person to give you a tour of the organization's headquarters or physical plant and an overview of the organization's operations.

Next imagine that you are going to conduct an organizational diagnosis. What have you learned during your scouting that relates to items #1 and #2 in the interpretive questions listed in the chapter? Pay particular attention to the way your contact person defined the organization's problems and strengths. Do any alternative interpretations occur to you? Summarize your experiences and understandings so far in a report on the following topics:

1. Description of the organization and the contact person (including source of access to them).
2. Initial contacts—including your feelings and behavior and those of the contact person.
3. Your contact person's view of the organization's strengths, weaknesses, current problems, desired state.
4. Your understanding of these issues.
5. Preliminary thoughts about conducting a diagnosis—topics, methods, groups, and individuals to be included.

2

Using the Open System Model

Two models, one that views organizations as open systems, and one that views them as political arenas, can help practitioners choose topics for diagnosis, develop criteria for assessing organizational effectiveness, and decide what steps, if any, will help clients solve problems and enhance effectiveness. A list of basic organizational information to gather at the start of a diagnosis is provided and methods are discussed for gathering and analyzing data in both broad and focused diagnoses.

VIEWING THE ORGANIZATION AS AN OPEN SYSTEM

The open system approach provides a general model that can guide the diagnosis of entire organizations and of divisions or departments within organizations (Beer, 1980; Daft, 1992; Katz & Kahn, 1978; Nadler & Tushman, 1989). Figure 2.1 presents a particularly useful version of the open system model.

System Elements

The main elements in the model and their key subcomponents are:

Inputs (or Resources):—raw materials, money, people (human resources), equipment, information, knowledge, and legal authorizations that an organization obtains from its environment and that contribute to the creation of its outputs.

Outputs:—products, services, and ideas that are the outcomes of organizational action. An organization transfers its main outputs back to the environment and uses others internally.

Technology:—tools, machines, and techniques for transforming resources into outputs. Techniques can be mental (e.g., exercising medical judgment) and social (e.g., psychotherapy), as well as chemical (e.g., drug therapy), physical (e.g., physiotherapy), mechanical (e.g., implanting artificial organ), or electronic (e.g., computerized heart monitor).

Environment:—The *task environment* includes all the external organizations and conditions that are directly related to an organization's main opera-

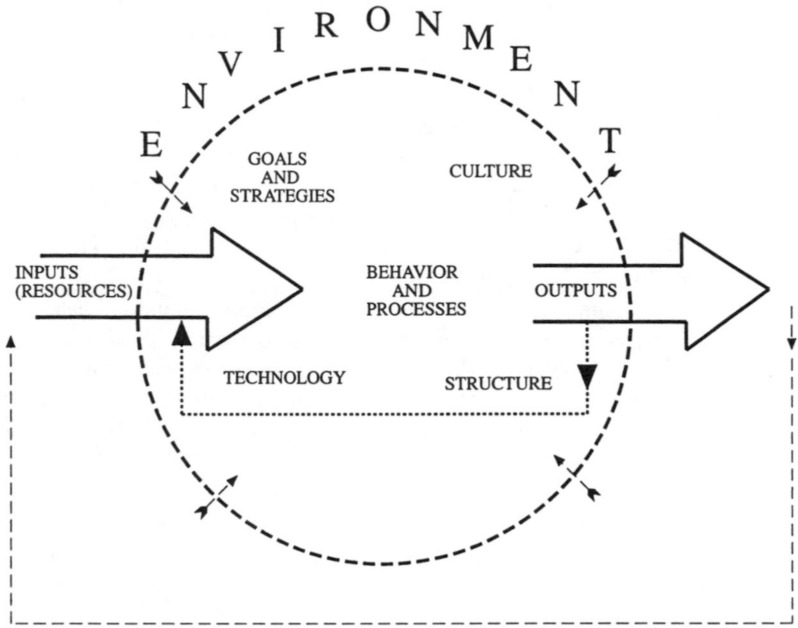

Figure 2.1. Organizations as Open Systems

tions and its technologies. They include funding sources, suppliers, distributors, unions, customers, clients, regulators, competitors, collaborative partners (e.g., in joint manufacturing ventures), markets for products and resources, and the state of knowledge concerning the organization's technologies. The *general environment* includes institutions and conditions having infrequent or long-term impacts on the organization and its task environment, including the economy, the legal system, the state of scientific and technical knowledge, social institutions such as the family, population distribution and composition, the political system, and the local or national cultures within which the organization operates.

Goals and strategies:—future states sought by the organization's dominant decision makers. *Goals* are desired end states (e.g., becoming the leading construction firm in the south), while *objectives* are specific targets and indicators of goal attainment (e.g., 5% growth per year). *Strategies* are overall routes to goals, including ways of dealing with the environment (e.g., strategy for expanding operations into shopping-mall construction business). *Plans* specify courses of action toward an end. Goals and strategies are the outcomes of conflict and negotiation among powerful parties within and outside the organization. Goals and other desired future states can be explicitly stated by decision makers or may be inferred from their actions.

Behavior and processes:—prevailing patterns of behavior, interactions, and relations between groups and individuals—including cooperation, conflict, coordination, communication, controlling and rewarding behavior, influence and power relations, supervision, leadership, decision making, problem solving, goal setting, information gathering, self-criticism, evaluation, and group learning.

Culture:—shared norms, values, beliefs and assumptions, and the behavior and artifacts that express these orientations—including symbols, rituals, stories, and language. Culture includes norms and understandings about the nature and identity of the organization, the way work is done, the value and possibility of changing or innovating, relations between lower and higher ranking members, and the nature of the environment.

Structure:—enduring relations between individuals, groups, and larger units—including role assignments (job descriptions; authority, responsibility, privileges attached to positions); grouping of positions in divisions, departments, and other units; standard operating procedures; established mechanisms for handling key processes such as coordination (e.g., committees, weekly meetings); human resource mechanisms (career lines, rewards, evaluation procedures); and actual patterns (e.g., informal relations, cliques, coalitions, power distribution) that may differ from officially mandated ones.

Key Features of the Model

The model contains several important ideas for diagnosis:

1. *External conditions influence the flow of inputs (resources) to organizations, affect the reception of outputs, and can directly affect internal operations*—for instance, when regulatory agencies define standards for safety, packaging, or advertising. Figure 2.1 depicts the possibility for direct effects on internal operations by showing a broken, permeable boundary around the organization. The external feedback loop depicts environmental responses to products or services that affect inputs—for example, reduced demand for cigarettes as a result of consumer recognition of the risks of smoking.

2. *Organizations use many of their products, services, and ideas as inputs to organizational maintenance or growth.* This feature is shown in Figure 2.1 by the feedback loop within the organizational boundary.

A computer firm uses its own machines and software; a university employs some of its doctoral students as instructors. Individual and group outcomes (chapter 3) also feed back into the organization.

3. *Organizations are influenced by their members as well as their environments.* Employee actions can reinforce or alter current practices. Change can result from visible pressure (e.g., union protests) and from hidden deals and alliances. Change can also occur incrementally and almost imperceptibly as people reinterpret their jobs and their work environments.

4. *The eight system elements and their subcomponents are interrelated and influence one another.* Thus developments within one element, such as technology, can have consequences for other elements (e.g., behavior, environmental relations). Links between elements need not be obvious or intended—for example, the acquisition of new computer networking capacity leads to redefinition of departmental objectives, tasks, and job descriptions.

5. *Organizations are constantly changing.*[1] *Reactive change* occurs in response to internal or external problems, while *anticipatory (proactive) change* aims at improving environmental standing or internal operations before problems arise. *Incremental changes* do not alter the main features of the eight system elements, whereas *strategic changes* entail basic changes in one or more critical elements—such as goals, environment, or culture—and in relations among these elements (Harrison & Phillips, 1991; Newman, Nadler, & Tushman, 1988). Both types of change contribute to system dynamics—growth, contraction, and changing levels of efficiency and effectiveness.

6. *An organization's success depends heavily on its ability to adapt to its environment—or to find a favorable environment in which to operate—as well as to tie people into their roles in the organization, conduct its transformative processes, and manage its operations* (Katz & Kahn, 1978). These system needs do not necessarily correspond to the interests or priorities of top management.

7. *Any level or unit within an organization can be viewed as a system.* When the system model is applied to a division or even to a single operating unit within a larger organization, other units within the organization will constitute much or all of the focal unit's task environment. Viewing units as systems facilitates diagnostic comparisons between them.

1. The assumption that systems seek a state of balance has been widely criticized (e.g., Abrahamsson, 1977) and has been avoided here.

The Model as a Diagnostic Guide

The system model reminds practitioners to consider all major system elements when conducting a diagnosis and not just to concentrate on topics such as morale or staff relations that seem initially to be important or easy to study. By referring to the model, both managers and consultants may better resist the appeals of management fads that attribute organizational success to one or two crucial features—such as quality, leadership, or culture. The system model also points to important interactions between system elements and can guide the assessment of how well these elements fit together (see chapter 4).

To give the diagnosis a broad focus, practitioners should find out what combination of system features has contributed to organizational success in the past and what changes in system features might threaten past successes. Case 6 illustrates this type of analysis for CHF, the organization described in Case 5.

Case 6

> Interviews suggested that until recently CHF had successfully provided a narrow range of health services. This past success rested substantially on the dedication of the nurses and medical aides, who persevered even though their work was neither challenging, well paid, nor prestigious. Many long-standing employees had strong ties to a local ethnic and religious subcommunity and had few alternative sources of local employment. These employees shared values that defined hospital work as fulfilling their moral obligation to care for people in need. The veteran employees were aging and were gradually being replaced by younger staff members who were less tied to the local community, less committed to its religious values, and less dedicated to their work. As a result turnover was rising, and CHF was having difficulties recruiting nurses and medical aides.

If developments within the organization or its environment are eroding the basis for past successes, consultants and clients must decide whether incremental adjustments in one or more system elements will preserve or enhance effectiveness or whether more fundamental, strategic changes are needed. Then clients and consultants can seek feasible routes to either form of improvement.

Besides guiding broad diagnoses, the system model can help practitioners focus on a particular organizational feature, such as human resource practices, or on a particular presented problem, such as staff tensions stemming from the merger of two firms. By scanning the system characteristics of the client organization, practitioners can better understand the context of the focal problem or issue and more readily define the diagnostic problem. Then they can concentrate their data gathering on those system elements and subcomponents most directly related to the focal problem.

When gathering and analyzing data for a focused diagnosis, practitioners should examine the impacts of all eight system elements on the focal problem. They may thus help clients break out of familiar ways of interpreting problems and discover more feasible solutions than those previously considered. Suppose, for example, that the customers and management of a resort hotel complain about the quality of guest service. The hotel manager attributes the problem to the hotel's inability to recruit experienced staff (a problem with human resource inputs), which stems from noncompetitive wage rates (a structural feature). By looking for links between the presented problem and other system elements, the consultant might find weaknesses in employee training programs and definitions of job responsibilities (additional structural features), the use of outmoded equipment (technology), and inadequate procedures for coordinating and controlling the work (processes). Improvements in these areas could enhance the quality of employee service, regardless of the employees' past work experience.

Redefining Presented Problems

The system model can also help practitioners redefine the problems or challenges initially presented by clients. Redefinition occurs whenever consultants treat problems presented as symptoms of broader or more fundamental conditions. The decision to examine all system elements in a broad diagnosis includes an assumption that the forces shaping organizational effectiveness may lie beyond the issues initially presented by the client. In the CHF study (cases 5 and 6), the practitioner assumed that the proposed organizational transformation could only succeed if the entire system changed. Hence he investigated system features that were not originally specified by the clients. Moreover, the consultant closely examined organizational leadership—a feature that was not discussed by the clients—because of the crucial role of leadership in transformation.

Although helpful, the open system model will not suggest precisely how to redefine a problem or how to go about solving it. Insights will typically derive more from past consulting experience and training, from ideas generated by members of the organization, and from the leads provided by some of the more explicit diagnostic models discussed in subsequent chapters.

GATHERING AND ANALYZING DATA

Basic Organizational Information

Drawing on the open system model (and on Levinson, 1972, pp. 55-59), we generated the following list of basic information about a client organization (or subunit) to gather during the scouting phase of diagnosis and the start of the data-gathering stage:

1. *Outputs:* mix and quantities of main products/services; rough quality indications such as reputation, ratings; indications of human "outputs," such as absenteeism, turnover, safety.
2. *Goals and strategies:* official statements of goals and mission; actual priorities as indicated by budget allocations to divisions, programs (e.g., percentage of budget allocated to research and development); preference for self-contained operations (within the organization) versus purchasing external goods and services, or forming links with other organizations (chapter 4).
3. *Inputs:* revenues and allocations from sales/services/funding sources (e.g., for agencies); financial assets, capital assets including real estate, physical plant, equipment (amount, condition, e.g., age, degree of obsolescence, state of repair); human resources—numbers of employees by job category, social and educational backgrounds, training, and previous experience.
4. *Environment:* affiliation and ownership (public versus private, affiliation with larger bodies and nature of relations with them); links with external organizations (legal agreements and informal traditions of cooperation); main organizations and conditions in task environment; availability of funds for growth and expansion (internal and external borrowing, grants and budget prospects for public agencies); physical and social surroundings (e.g., city center or suburban location, transportation, access to services, neighborhood safety).
5. *Technology:* type of production (unit, batch, mass, continuous process), level of automation, use of management information systems, office computeriza-

tion; procedures used to treat or process people in service organizations; data on operational failures, accidents, wastage, down time.

6. *Structure:* major divisions and units; number of levels of hierarchy; basis for grouping of units (e.g., by functions, markets), coordination mechanisms; spans of control; spatial distribution of units, employees and activities; unions and other forms of employee representation, labor contracts, grievance procedures, human resource policies and practices; formal obligations affecting operations (e.g., affirmative action rules, quality assurance standards); prominent power blocks and coalitions.
7. *Behavior and processes:* main patterns of high-level decision making, strategy formulation, and planning; major types of conflicts such as labor relations, conflicts between divisions; strength of unions and degree of militancy, employee involvement in issues other than compensation; communication styles (e.g., oral, written, meeting oriented).
8. *Culture:* symbols of organizational identity (logo, slogans, advertising campaigns, physical appearance of corporate headquarters and branches); myths (stories of founders, historic successes); rituals (outings, celebrations, annual reviews and plans); jargon (frequently used terms and phrases); dominant styles of dress, decor, lifestyle; clients' work styles (e.g., taking work home, working overtime).
9. *System dynamics:* life-cycle stage: entrepreneurial, collectivity, formalization, structural elaboration (Quinn & Cameron, 1983); overall financial condition—profits, losses, deficits; growth and contraction in key system elements (e.g., layoffs, sell-offs; budget changes); major changes in any system element.

Statistics on topics such as budgets, workforce composition, financial position, and the scope of operations appear in organizational documents or can be prepared by staff members of the client organization after the completion of the study contract. Whenever available, practitioners should also obtain official statements of the organization's mission and goals, charts of the organizational structure, and organizational histories. Site visits can provide some impressions of the organizational culture, such as the corporate image presented by buildings, equipment, and furnishings (e.g., state of the art or solid and traditional). Practitioners can also note the ways that employees dress, use jargon and terminology, and arrange their offices and work spaces (Steele, 1973). Subsequent investigations will be needed, however, to determine whether these artifacts and behavior patterns reflect everyday practice and underlying norms and values (Rousseau, 1990; Schein, 1985).

High-level managers or their assistants are usually asked to provide additional basic information. Interviews with top managers, heads of departments or divisions, and a sample of other members can provide more adequate data on system features that were not adequately covered initially, such as organizational processes or members' assessments of how well things work in the organization. A schedule such as in the General Orientation Interview (Appendix A) covers characteristics of units and some broader organizational factors. Alternatively, investigators can construct a schedule that concentrates on organization-wide features. Standardized questions covering many of the topics listed under Basic Organizational Information as well as other important organizational features appear in the schedules of the International Organizational Observatory and the National Organizations Study described in Appendix B. Investigators can also follow the procedure explained in chapter 5 to construct an *interview guide* to use in semistructured interviews.

Measurement Problems

Since some of the factors covered in the Basic Organizational Information and General Orientation Interview are abstract and hard to measure, practitioners must often content themselves with nonrigorous measures. For instance, when analyzing basic information about the organizational culture of a firm, a practitioner might make a judgment about the orientation toward employees conveyed in newsletters or other documents (e.g., hard-nosed and competitive or caring and supportive) without systematically coding the contents of the documents or interviewing managers and employees about human resource policies. More rigorous but time-consuming methods of gathering data should be contemplated only if the topic is particularly critical to the diagnosis. Likewise, practitioners often have to settle for global assessments of very complex conditions. When interviewing top management, for example, practitioners could ask for general assessments of the organization's overall financial condition (ranging from excellent to critical), the competitiveness of the environment, and its degree of threat or munificence.

Consultants can learn a great deal about their respondents' viewpoints and can identify controversial or problematic issues for further study by comparing their respondents' interpretations of complex organizational and environmental conditions. To bring out underlying interpretations and assumptions, practitioners can ask respondents to describe the history of their organization (Leach, 1979) or the nature and causes of major organizational successes and failures (Argyris and Schon, 1978, pp. 32-48). Consultants can also gain insights about respondents' views by comparing their descriptions of ostensibly objective phenomena, such as the lines of authority and reporting. If, for example, departmental managers draw different organization charts of the same division, this diversity points to ambiguity and possibly to conflict about the lines of authority and the division of labor in that division. By using two or more types of data on the same topic (e.g., descriptions of corporate goals in the report to stockholders and in interviews), practitioners can also illuminate the perspectives and concerns of individuals and groups and can develop their own, independent judgments about topics on which participants hold divergent views.

Summarizing and Analyzing Data

The lists of Basic Organizational Information and System Elements can serve as accounting schemes for organizing and summarizing diagnostic findings. One straightforward approach is to make a separate card or file for each system element and to enter information into appropriate files, cross-referencing them as needed, and noting the source of the information. A typical entry in the technology file for a diagnostic study of a high school might read as follows:

> *Teaching techniques and equipment:* Most classes are lectures and discussions conducted by teacher, supplemented by homework exercises and projects. Remedial coaching and computer-assisted instruction available in math and English. Laboratories in sciences use microscopes, prepared slides, models, charts, Bunsen burners, ring stands, chemicals. Microcomputer lab for wordprocessing after school and elective courses in programming. Two language laboratories per week in French and Spanish. Minimal use of audiovisual equipment, field trips in humanities, social sciences.
>
> *Administrative:* Filing is manual; electric and manual typewriters, photocopier, mimeograph in office; two phone lines, fax machine in principal's office. *Source:* Assistant Principal.

Popular wordprocessing and database-management programs, as well as programs designed for qualitative analysis (Fielding & Lee, 1992), can greatly facilitate the filing and analysis of diagnostic findings.

Except in very small organizations, divisions and other major subunits will probably differ substantially from one another in terms of features such as technology, structure, and processes. In addition, each major subunit usually deals with a different subenvironment within the organization's task environment. Hence, summaries should note the distinctive profiles of each division as well as features common to the whole organization.

To summarize responses to interviews based on a schedule such as the General Orientation Interview, practitioners can start by grouping together responses to each question that make the same point and then record each type of response and the number of people giving it. If, for example, 10 employees in a branch of a fast-food chain were interviewed, a typical entry in the summary might read:

> Are there any difficulties or barriers to getting work done here or doing it the way you'd like to ? (You can mention more than one.)
>
> - Annoying customer complaints about food—taste, quality, etc. (3)
> - Pressures from supervisor to work faster, come in on weekends (2)
> - We often run out of buns or ketchup (4)
> - Loud, disruptive customers (2)
> - Sexual harassment by customers (3)
> - No problems (3)

Practitioners can present the entire range of responses to specific questions as feedback to stimulate analysis of the operations and suggestions for improvement or they can aggregate and summarize findings using accounting schemes such as the one derived from the system model. They can then present an overview of organizational strengths and problems in a feedback report. In the fast-food study above, if the supervisor were to receive the feedback, the consultant would probably prefer the latter method to avoid identifying the two people who complained about their supervisor.

The system model can also be used to analyze the interactions between system elements. A graphic approach that aids both analysis and feedback is to place the eight elements in a circle and list their important subcomponents—for example, processes such as rewarding, controlling, and conflict management. Color-coded lines can be drawn between system elements or subcomponents that promote a focal condition, such as job satisfaction, and those that hinder it. Data supporting the inferences in the figure can be recorded separately and used appropriately in feedback. Investigators can diagnose environmental relations in terms of the effectiveness of current responses to the environment and the ability of the organization to deal with anticipated external developments. The next three chapters provide more guidelines to diagnosing the organization as a system.

CHOOSING EFFECTIVENESS CRITERIA

A bewildering range of choices faces anyone seeking to define and measure organizational effectiveness. The system model can help guide these choices. However, to assess effectiveness and the feasibility of change, practitioners need to draw upon an additional model that treats organizations as political arenas (see chapter 4; Cobb, 1986; Greiner & Schein, 1988; Shirom, 1993a). The political model of organizations draws attention to the divergent stakeholders (or constituencies) in and around organizations. Stakeholders are groups and individuals affected by a decision or a project who seek to influence decisions in keeping with their own interests, goals, priorities, and understandings (Hall, 1987; Ramirez & Bartunek, 1989; Rossi & Freeman, 1993, pp. 100-111, 406-420). As a result of their divergent interests and views, organizational subgroups from distinct fields, functions, and ranks often advocate different ways of judging organizational success and effectiveness.

Types of Criteria

Table 2.1 groups the many criteria used to assess organizational effectiveness into three broad categories (see Cameron, 1980; Hall, 1987; Kanter & Brinkerhoff, 1981). These criteria derive from different images of preferred organizational states and reflect divergent assumptions about the conditions that promote these desired states.

Output-goal criteria correspond to many of the specific targets toward which members of organizations strive. They are sometimes expressed in terms of the success or failure to achieve a particular end, such as the design of a solar-powered vehicle or the development of a workable plan for rezoning a city district. Criteria dealing with output goals are most useful when participants and practitioners can define goals in terms of clear, measurable objectives and members of the client organization agree on the meaning and importance of these goals. This type of criterion is often hard to use in service and cultural organizations. Even if decision makers and other stakeholders in these organizations agree on some abstract goal, such as improving public health,

Table 2.1
Effectiveness Criteria

Type	*Operational Definitions*
(1) *Output Goals*	
Goal Attainment	Success/Failure (e.g., rocket launching).
Quantity of Outputs	Productivity (units produced, hours of services provided, values of sales, services—sometimes per work unit or per time period); profits (revenues minus costs); revenues as percentage of investment; percentage of target group reached by services, messages.
Quality of Outputs	Number of rejects, returns, complaints; client, customer satisfaction; expert rating of services (e.g., in health education) or work performance (e.g., in manufacturing, military); impact of services or products on target population (e.g., impact of anti-litter campaign).
(2) *Internal System State*	
Costs of Production or Services	Efficiency (ratio of output value to costs such as labor, equipment, with constant quality); wastage, downtime.
Human Outcomes	Employee satisfaction with pay, working conditions and relations; motivation (disposition to work); work effort (observed, reported); low absenteeism, lateness, and turnover; health and safety of workforce.
Consensus/Conflict	Agreement on goals and procedures; cohesion (mutual attraction, identification with work group, and organization); cooperation (reported/observed) within and between units; few strikes, work stoppages, dispute, and feuds.
Work and Information Flows	Smooth flow of products, ideas and information; few snags, foul-ups, misunderstandings; rich, multidirectional communication, accurate analysis of information.
Interpersonal Relations	High levels of trust; open communication of feelings, needs between ranks; deemphasis of status differences.
Participation	Subordinates participate in making decisions affecting them; diffusion of power and authority.
Fit	Compatibility of requirements of system elements (see chapter 4).
(3) *Adaptation and Resource Position*	
Resources-quantity	Size of organization (employees; cash, physical assets); resource flows (e.g., investment, grants and budget support in nonprofit organizations).
Resources-quality	Human capital (experience and training of employees); desirability of clients (e.g., selectiveness of college admissions); reputation of staff.

(Continued)

Table 2.1
Continued

Type	*Operational Definitions*
Legitimacy	Support and approval by community and public bodies; public image; compliance with standards of legal, regulatory, professional bodies (e.g., government pollution control standards, accreditation of college).
Competitive/ Strategic Position	Market share, ranking among competitors in size, volume of business; reputation within the field of industry; full use of capacities to exploit external opportunities.
Impact on Environment	Ability to shape demand, government action, behavior of competitors, suppliers.
Adaptiveness	Adjustment to changes in inputs and demands for outputs; flexibility in handling crises, surprises.
Innovativeness	Number, quality of new products, services, procedures; incorporation of new technologies, management practices.
Fit	Compatibility of internal system elements with requirements, constraints of environment.

they are likely to differ on the operational meaning and measurement of the goal. An additional drawback to defining effectiveness solely in terms of output goals is that this approach tends to confine the consultant to the role of a technical evaluator.

Many of the criteria in the second category of Table 2.1 refer to *internal organizational states and processes* that can contribute to achieving output goals, while others, such as employee welfare or satisfaction, are sometimes regarded as ends in themselves. Efficiency and cost-related criteria are hard to apply to not-for-profit organizations because of the difficulties in measuring all of the important aspects of outputs and inputs. In contrast, practitioners can apply the system criteria relating to internal relations and processes to any type of organization. These criteria can be thought of as desirable states or as indicators of a more global state of organizational health (e.g., Beckhard, 1969) that facilitates coping with organizational challenges. Criteria relating to smooth internal processes and cooperative relations are particularly appropriate wherever work requires high levels of mutual consultation and adjustment, for instance, in professional and management teams.

Criteria concerning internal system states are also applicable to the diagnosis of operations within departments or subunits that have little control over their environments.

The major drawback to these internal system criteria is that they may lead practitioners and clients to underestimate the potential contribution of internal pluralism, tension, and conflict to the process of organizational change and adaptation. Conflict may be too low, rather than too high, if work standards are lax, if members submit automatically to authority, or if they avoid confronting the challenges and problems facing their organization (Robbins, 1978).

Besides being applicable to for-profit firms, many of the *adaptation and resource-position criteria* are applicable to not-for-profit organizations, which frequently have unclear output goals. Even not-for-profit organizations operate as open systems that compete for funds, personnel, and other scarce resources and face pressures to adapt to changing external conditions. Criteria such as adaptiveness are particularly relevant to organizations facing rapidly changing environments, as in the case of firms undergoing globalization of markets or nonprofit organizations vulnerable to changes in public support, governmental regulations, and funding procedures.

During financial crises, adaptation and resource acquisition become life-and-death matters. In some organizational crises, the bodies that fund, license, or sponsor an organization may question its right to exist. In these cases, effectiveness criteria relating to legitimacy become central. The adaptation and resource position criteria are easier to apply in diagnoses where practitioners work with high-level administrators who have the authority to try to improve the environmental standing of an entire organization or semi-autonomous division.

Comparison Standards

In choosing and developing working definitions of effectiveness, consultants must decide what time frames and comparison standards to use (Cameron, 1980). They can compare:

- current and past levels of effectiveness, for example, rates of growth, and development.
- the effectiveness of units within the same organization, for example, comparisons of efficiency ratings, accidents, quality.
- the client organization's effectiveness to that of others in the same industry or field, for example, comparisons of profitability or sales to industry figures.
- the organization's current state in relation to some minimum standard, such as conformity to federal environmental standards.

- the current state to an ideal standard, such as innovativeness or community service.

The time frame used can vary from hours or days to several years, depending in part on the organizational feature being assessed. Different time frames can also be applied to the same feature. A service or manufacturing firm's performance might seem impressive, for example, if we look at its current quarterly profits or return on investment. In contrast, if the firm achieves these results by cutting costs and aggressively marketing its services or products, it may be unable to sustain these results for more than a year or two because of a lack of investment in the development of new products and services (Hayes & Abernathy, 1980).

Conflicts Among Effectiveness Criteria

Close inspection will reveal many contradictions and tensions among the criteria listed in Table 2.1 (Hall, 1987). For example, growth usually indicates that an organization is successful in obtaining needed resources, but growth can also lead to less participation in decision making, reduced efficiency, and less ability to adjust to environmental changes. People can hold conflicting priorities and evaluative criteria without being aware of the conflicts because they do not evoke the criteria simultaneously or spell out their operational implications.

An additional problem is that few effectiveness criteria equally suit the interests and priorities of all organizational members and stakeholders. The owners of shares in an electric utility, for example, will probably assess effectiveness in terms of short-term profits. But environmental groups judge the utility by its impact on air and water quality, and the utilities commission looks for conformity to regulations covering rate setting and reporting of data on operations. Within the firm the development group calls for investments that will support innovation and growth in the long run, while employee representatives press for better wages and working conditions. Similar divergences occur in not-for-profit organizations (Kanter & Summers, 1987). Hence, the effectiveness criteria that best reflect the interests and needs of one subgroup, such as the dominant decision makers within the top management, will probably neglect the priorities of less powerful managers, external clients, unskilled workers, government regulators, and so on.

How to Choose Effectiveness Criteria

If the various effectiveness criteria are not mutually compatible and applicable, how should consultants choose appropriate criteria and incorporate them into diagnosis? To make these decisions they need to consider three sets of questions (Cameron, 1984; Campbell,1977; Connolly & Deutsch, 1980; Goodman & Pennings, 1980):

1. Who are the main clients for the study; what do they regard as the preferred state of the organization; and what criteria reflect the degree of attainment of this state? How can the consultant help clients resolve conflicts and ambiguities among their stated preferences?
2. What other states or conditions will help promote client goals or are otherwise appropriate as effectiveness criteria? How can consultants encourage clients to adopt these additional criteria?
3. What effectiveness criteria are favored by other stakeholders—including clients, employees, members of external units and organizations? How well does the organization meet these standards? Are there criteria about which all powerful stakeholders can agree?

Identifying Clients and Clarifying Their Priorities

The main clients for a diagnosis are those people who have responsibility for deciding what actions (if any) to take in light of the diagnostic findings and for planning and implementing such actions. If clients and stakeholders hold ambiguous or internally inconsistent views of what is best for their organization, practitioners need to decide whether these inconsistencies harm the organization. In some cases organizations flourish while pursuing conflicting goals and applying conflicting standards of effectiveness (Cameron & Quinn, 1988)—such as product quality and cost reduction (Eisenhardt & Westcott, 1988).

Consultants can deal with conflicts between clients and other stakeholders about effectiveness by asking clients to develop a working consensus about organizational priorities so as to provide the consultant with guidelines for choosing effectiveness criteria (e.g., Beckhard & Harris, 1977). Clients can then meet to define their priorities for the diagnosis with or without the help of the consultant. If this approach is impractical, consultants may have to accept the goals and priorities of the most powerful clients and seek ways of achieving them that will bring benefits to the broadest possible spectrum of members and stakeholders.

Consultants can also help resolve conflicts and ambiguities about effectiveness criteria by examining the criteria that powerful clients use in practice. For example, to determine whether top management actually treats innovativeness as an important facet of effectiveness, consultants can assess whether management rewards people and groups for innovation. Moreover, consultants can examine whether management provides the conditions needed for innovation, including investment in research and development and discretionary funds for new projects (Delbecq & Mills, 1985).

When practitioners examine the priorities underlying major decisions, resource allocations, and patterns of rewarding and evaluating performance, they may find that their clients' operative goals and standards diverge greatly from their stated priorities. If consultants discover major discrepancies between declared and operative priorities early in a diagnosis, they may present their findings to clients and help them to rework their priorities and conceptions of effectiveness in light of the feedback or to redouble their efforts to achieve their initially stated goals. This process of providing feedback about group goals and priorities can sometimes become a major focus of intervention aimed at helping clients clarify their goals, priorities, policies, and evaluative criteria. In client-oriented diagnosis, the process of examining and clarifying priorities can occur quite naturally as consultants and clients collaborate in choosing effectiveness criteria during the design and analysis phases.

Choosing Additional Criteria

In most diagnoses consultants introduce additional effectiveness criteria that do not derive directly from initial client priorities but point to conditions (such as teamwork or flexibility) that can contribute to the achievement of clients' goals or are generally compatible with the clients' image of the desired state of the organization. Sometimes consultants also lead clients toward a radically different image of what is good for their organization—for example, by suggesting that if the organization does not become more responsive to the requirements of its clients or customers, it will soon lose their business and run into difficulty attracting new customers.

By introducing effectiveness criteria relating to the organization's internal system state and its ability to obtain resources and adapt to its environment, practitioners may help their clients redefine specific problems and challenges in terms of needs for improving broader, underlying forms of effectiveness. If these broader aspects of effectiveness are enhanced, the organization will be more able to handle future problems, as well as coping with current ones. For example, enhancing the satisfaction and motivation of workers can help reduce such immediate signs of dissatisfaction as rapid employee turnover, absenteeism, and noncompliance with minimal performance requirements. But improving quality of work life, satisfaction, and motivation can also yield longterm benefits such as a loyal, flexible workforce.

Developing Consensual Criteria

Consultants can sometimes avoid problems raised by conflicts among effectiveness criteria by concentrating on one or more criteria about which powerful stakeholders can reach agreement. For example, when organizations decline or undergo crises, otherwise conflicting groups may agree on the common goal of survival. Agreement around this goal can then lay the foundation for choosing effectiveness criteria that reflect the organization's capacity to survive and undergo renewal. Likewise, stakeholders sometimes find it easier to agree on the signs of *ineffectiveness* and the need to combat them than on the meaning and measurement of effectiveness (Cameron, 1984). Consultants can contribute to the development of agreement about appropriate diagnostic criteria by providing stakeholders with data about the costs of ineffective practices or the risks of failures to improve effectiveness. Moreover, consultants can help build consensus about effectiveness if they can discover routes to organizational improvement that will benefit most of the powerful stakeholders, rather than benefiting one group at the expense of another.

Using Multiple Criteria

Instead of defining consensual criteria, consultants can adapt a *multi-constituency approach* (Kanter & Summers, 1987; Tsui, 1990; Zammuto, 1984) that defines effectiveness in terms of the organization's ability to satisfy its diverse constituencies (Connolly & Deutsch, 1980). This approach treats the differences of goals and interpretations among subgroups as legitimate and normal and makes no effort to resolve the resultant differences among effectiveness criteria. Instead, practitioners develop measures of effectiveness that reflect the divergent priorities of key stakeholders, assess the organization in terms of these measures, and provide clients with feedback on how well they are meeting these divergent standards. Although such data can be very informative, they do not usually yield clear implications for action.

The choice of effectiveness criteria in diagnosis ultimately depends on the specific needs and character of the client organization and the goals of the diagnostic study. In many cases, several criteria can be used during data gathering. Their order of importance can be decided upon during the analysis of the findings and the formulation of plans for action. Whatever approach practitioners take, they should try to reach an understanding with clients as early as possible about the effectiveness criteria, time frames, and comparison standards to be used. By doing so, practitioners increase the chances that clients will regard the diagnostic data and recommendations as worthwhile and useful.

Problems of Measuring Effectiveness

In principle, the procedure for developing systematic measures of effectiveness is identical to that of developing any measure (Judd et al., 1991). After clarifying the concept, the investigator specifies what phenomena will be considered indicative of effectiveness and chooses measures that fit this operational definition. The following example shows how the initial conceptualization of effectiveness affects subsequent choices:

Conceptualization A: Effectiveness refers (in part) to the absence of rancorous conflict among the people and groups that contribute to work flow.

Operational definition: absence of conflicts that interrupt work flow.

Possible measures: number of days lost to strikes and number of work stoppages.

Conceptualization B: Effectiveness refers to smooth work flow.

Operational definition: absence of all types of interruptions in the work flow.

Possible measures: amount of time that units are idle waiting for inputs; number of interruptions; total time to produce a product or complete some operation (e.g., develop marketing plan).

In practice, consultants often have to define and measure effectiveness in ways that allow them to analyze data that are available or can be gathered quickly and inexpensively. Unless they keep in mind clear conceptual and operational definitions of effectiveness when working with less-than-perfect data, they may interpret their findings incorrectly and overlook important phenomena that are not covered by these measures. For example, data on pupils' performance on standardized achievement tests might be readily available to consultants conducting a diagnosis of an elementary school. Unfortunately, these tests do not measure many important educational outcomes, such as the ability to engage in self-study, critical thinking, and creativity. Yet these kinds of outcomes and the social and educational processes occurring within the school might be more relevant to the diagnosis than the outcomes measured by the standardized tests. A further problem arises when available data were originally designed to evaluate the performance of employees or units. In such cases, members may have learned to perform in ways that make them look good on the measured criteria—such as the number of sales—while neglecting other desirable forms of behavior—such as customer satisfaction or service—that are less closely monitored (Lawler & Rhode, 1976).

Another issue in measuring effectiveness concerns the value of using objective, behavioral measures of effectiveness (e.g., number of strike days), rather than subjective measures that reflect the judgments of participants or experts (e.g., descriptions of the quality of labor relations in the plant). In practice, this distinction often turns out to be far from clear cut (Campbell, 1977, p. 45). For a health-maintenance organization, the number of patients treated per week, divided by the size of the staff, is an apparently objective measure of output. But we must have a standard—such as an average for strictly comparable organizations—to decide whether the figure is too high, too low, or about right. Even comparing the current performance of an organization to its past performance does not resolve the problem. Suppose the accounts in a bank grew by 5% over the previous year. Are these results substantial or lackluster in light of the efforts and investments made? In the final analysis, the kinds of objective data that managers collect and pay attention to and their evaluations of these figures depend heavily on their subjective priorities and standards.

ASSESSING FEASIBILITY OF CHANGE AND CHOOSING APPROPRIATE INTERVENTIONS

The political and open system models can also help practitioners decide what steps, if any, will help clients solve problems and enhance organizational effectiveness.

Interpretive and Process Issues

To make such an assessment, practitioners need to consider the following issues (see also Burke, 1982, pp. 215-233; President and Fellows of Harvard, 1980):

1. Does the Organization Need Strategic Changes?

Top managers usually undertake strategic changes in response to external changes in markets and competition, technology, and in legal and regulatory actions. Less frequently, strategic changes anticipate such developments. Typical strategic changes include mergers, internal structural reorganizations, major cutbacks or investment programs, fundamental changes in rules and processes (e.g., programs for Total Quality Management), and upgrading of major technologies. Such steps are hard to accomplish and entail substantial risk since they usually require major investments or reallocations of budgets and can have widespread, unanticipated consequences throughout the organization.

Strategic changes are often initiated by new owners and managers rather than by consultants. Assuming a leadership role, the heads of an organization may seek to transform it by redefining its goals, strategies, and culture (Nadler & Tushman, 1989; Tichy & DeVanna, 1986). Practitioners of diagnosis can help such clients assess the feasibility of proposed changes (e.g., Case 5), find the best ways to implement them (e.g., Case 1), and monitor progress toward implementation (Johnson, Hoskisson, & Margulies, 1990).

Strategic changes are needed when an organization undergoes *decline* (Whetten, 1987)—in the sense of a continuing drop in key resource flows—or is very likely to decline without suitable anticipatory action. Decline can stem from shrinkage within the industry or sector to which the organization belongs or from some particular action by the organization that harms its environmental standing (Cameron, Sutton, & Whetten, 1988).

Strategic change is also needed when incremental changes have become inadequate or are likely to become so in the near future. Troubleshooting procedures and other system adjustments are inadequate if an organization has fallen into a state of permanent crisis, lurching from one troubleshooting episode to another, or if the short-term solutions to crises create long-lasting havoc in the organization (Sayles, 1979, pp. 160-162). Moreover, organizations probably need strategic change if symptoms of ineffectiveness—such as quality problems, financial losses, operating inefficiencies, and customer dissatisfaction—persist or grow worse despite efforts to solve problems with quick and easy techniques.

By anticipating the need for strategic change, managers can more readily consider a range of possible actions and adjust their program for implementing change on the basis of preliminary feedback concerning implementation. In contrast, if managers attempt to make strategic changes only after their organization faces the threats of decline or outright crisis, they will probably have to work within extreme cash and time constraints.

2. *Is There Readiness for Change?*

Members of an organization and external stakeholders often realize that something must be done to change an organization when they face mounting signs of ineffectiveness such as declining sales, poor quality, eroding budget support, labor unrest, internal conflict, or failures to exploit opportunities. Diagnostic feedback may increase readiness for strategic changes as well as for incremental improvements, by bringing acute or widespread problems to the attention of clients and other stakeholders or by showing that these problems are more severe then people had thought.

3. How Will Internal and External Stakeholders React to Proposed Interventions?

Proposals for interventions to improve effectiveness can come from consultants, the clients, other members of the organization, and external stakeholders and controlling organizations. To assess the probable impacts of interventions, practitioners need to decide how the groups affected by the proposed steps are likely to react to them. In particular, consultants should try to determine whether key decision makers and other powerful constituencies support the proposed interventions and will provide the backing and resources needed to implement them or are likely to engage in defensive behavior (Ashforth & Lee, 1990) and to resist interventions. People often resist interventions that threaten their own objectives and interests, contradict their understandings of the right way to do their job, or undermine their power, prestige, and job security.

What if diagnosis reveals that a particular form of intervention will probably encounter serious resistance by clients or by internal or external stakeholders? In this case consultants can help clients look for ways to unfreeze resistance and build support for the proposed change (Chin & Benne, 1985). For instance, consultants and top managers can sometimes help rival power groups discover common interests—such as insuring competitiveness in the global marketplace—and work together toward mutually beneficial solutions. When specific interventions create resistance, clients and consultants should look for alternatives that can serve equally well as levers for change but are less threatening and better fit the needs and concerns of the affected groups (Harrison, 1970). Consultants might, for example, suggest that management retrain and reassign employees whose jobs will be eliminated by merging two divisions rather than firing these employees.

Unfortunately, implementing change often creates resistance. Unless organizations are growing vigorously, change usually requires the reallocation of current resources. During declines and crises, for example, immediate steps must be taken to reduce costs, improve cash flows, or restore public confidence and support. Strategic changes must follow these emergency measures. The redistribution of resources accompanying such changes almost invariably threatens some stakeholders in and around the organization and creates conflicts among them (Greenlagh, 1982). Emotions often run high during decline, political relations become more polarized, and managerial credibility drops (Cameron, Kim, & Whetten, 1987; Gray & Ariss, 1985; Krantz, 1985). Hence, resistance to change may become intense among both internal and external subgroups.

Under conditions like these, top management usually must impose change, rather than implementing it through participatory decision processes (Dunphy & Stace, 1988). Consultants to clients who must impose change can help them examine the possible effects of alternative ways of handling resistance—such as bargaining, threats, and sanctions to force compliance (Kotter & Schlesinger, 1979).

4. Does the Organization Have the Capacity to Implement Change?

In diagnosing prospects for change, practitioners also need to assess whether the client organization has the capacity to implement the proposed interventions. Capacity for change becomes particularly critical when organizations must undergo a lengthy transition before they can reach the desired future state (Beckhard & Harris, 1977). To make a preliminary assessment of implementation capacity, practitioners can check whether each element of the system is likely to make the contributions required for successful implementation. To find out, consultants can pose interpretive questions like these:

- Does the organization have the resources—people, funds, skills, knowledge—and technology needed to implement proposed interventions? Can it obtain or develop the resources it lacks?
- Can adjustments in current structural and technical arrangements accommodate and facilitate implementation (e.g., through the creation of teams or project groups to manage the change)?
- Will dominant behavior patterns, processes, beliefs, and values in the organizational culture fit those required by the change program?
- Will the environment provide the necessary support, permission, and resources?

5. Will the Proposed Interventions Achieve the Desired Results Without Having Undesirable Consequences?

Before recommending interventions, practitioners should make a final accounting of the probable benefits and risks of each possible move. By considering the likely impacts of proposed interventions on all system elements and on the interactions among them, consultants estimate whether the interventions are likely to have the desired consequences without creating other, unintended consequences that would undercut their benefits. Programs of change are more likely to succeed if they fit key conditions in the client organization, including:

- Members' characteristics (e.g., preferences for pay versus more vacation time)
- Organizational and technical conditions (e.g., equipment, division of labor)
- External constraints (e.g., consumer preferences)
- Organizational culture (informal norms, values, and beliefs)

In assessing capacity for change, practitioners make judgments about the probable fit between current practices and proposed changes (Schwartz & Davis, 1981). For instance, when two very different firms undertake a joint venture or merge their operations, gaps between the cultures of the firms can undermine relations between staff members from each firm (Buono & Bowditch, 1989).

Consultants should weigh carefully the likely positive and negative effects of any interventions that might produce lasting improvements in effectiveness. If time permits, they can recommend the beneficial interventions that are least likely to encounter serious resistance or have other undesirable consequences and that require the lowest levels of support and commitment from members (Harrison, 1970). If these steps succeed, more ambitious interventions can be considered subsequently. When time is short, consultants and clients must look for the interventions most likely to produce vital improvements and chart ways to handle any anticipated resistance.

Methodological Issues

Assessing Support and Resistance to Change

Since behavior cannot easily be predicted from attitudes (Fishbein & Ajzen, 1975), people's attitudes toward a proposed intervention are not good predictors of how they will act after the intervention is implemented. Social pressures from peers or supervisors can make people hesitate to reveal their true feelings. Moreover, people's initial attitudes toward a change may shift during its implementation as they discover that the costs and benefits of the change differ greatly from what they had anticipated. Despite these drawbacks, attitudinal data can reveal previously unnoticed hostility toward programs of change. In addition, interviews with powerful individuals who represent key constituencies may indicate whether they will support or resist an intervention. Influential leaders who lack formal authority should also be included in such interviews.

To move beyond attitudinal assessments, consultants can also examine the ways that members reacted in the past when changes were introduced. If practitioners and clients carefully consider the nature of past interventions and the procedures used to introduce these interventions, they may be able to learn what types of interventions are most feasible and which procedures are best for implementing them.

Evaluating Capacity, Readiness, and Consequences

The complexity of organizational relations and the indeterminacy of future behavior make it very difficult to anticipate people's reactions to interventions and their probable consequences. As a result, consultants and managers sometimes take a more experimental approach to implementation. They might, for instance, implement a program in stages, beginning with some preliminary activity (such as off-site meetings with top managers to plan changes) to learn from members' reactions to each stage how they may react to subsequent stages. By developing contingency plans for responding to possible developments at each stage, consultants and their clients can prepare appropriate steps to facilitate program implementation. Alternatively, management may introduce administrative or technological changes as experiments in one or more units within an organization. After a trial period and an assessment of the consequences, the innovation can be modified if necessary and then diffused to other parts of the organization. Managers often take this approach when introducing costly technological innovations such as robotics or trying out structural innovations. For example, the risks are high when manufacturing plants eliminate periodic quality control inspections and instead provide assembly workers with the training and equipment to inspect their own work (e.g., Eisenhardt & Westcott, 1988). Hence, plant managers may prefer to evaluate the procedure's impact on a single production line, before introducing it elsewhere. Unfortunately, managers in both the public and private sectors sometimes agree to introduce such a pilot program to show that they are forward looking, although they have little real intention of extending the program to the rest of the organization. An additional drawback to experimental programs is that the enthusiasm created by the newness and uniqueness of the program can wear off when the change is introduced widely and becomes well established.

EXERCISES

1. Effectiveness Criteria

Conduct an open, semistructured interview with one of the people in charge of an organization (or unit) to which you have access. First ask the person to describe an example of successful operations in the organization. Then ask what the general objectives are toward which the members should strive and how they know whether they are achieving them. Based on these responses and any other data (e.g., impressions from previous exercises):

1. Specify the effectiveness criteria to which the respondent referred.
2. Explain whether these criteria reflect considerations of output, system state, or adaptation.
3. Suggest additional effectiveness criteria that would fit the expressed priorities and needs of those in charge of the organization.
4. Note criteria that reflect the interests of other internal and external stakeholders and criteria on which consensus might be achieved. Explain your choices.

2. Resistance to Change

Talk with a manager or organizational authority who can describe the individuals and groups within the organization and those outside of it that have a stake in the decisions made by top management. Ask the manager to describe how these stakeholders would react to a particular intervention—a step that the manager thinks might help solve a problem or enhance effectiveness. Organize your data in a chart with a column for the stakeholders likely to support or cooperate with this change and a column for those likely to resist it. In parentheses rank each group as strong, moderate, or weak in terms of its potential impact on the organization. Write a summary describing your interview, the current balance of forces supporting the proposed intervention and opposing it, and the kinds of steps toward improvement that seem feasible in light of the forces shown in your table.

3. General Orientation Interviews

Plan a General Orientation Interview (see Appendix A) that concentrates on the specific unit (e.g., department) in which the person being interviewed works. Note in advance which questions are inappropriate and will be skipped (e.g., Section V) and which will need rewording to make them more applicable. Do not spend more than an hour on this first interview, even if you cannot cover all questions. Write a report in which you summarize the problems you encountered in conducting the interview (e.g., keeping the respondent on track, time pressures, skipped questions). Explain how you would handle the next interview. After getting feedback on your report from your instructor, conduct two more interviews with members of the same or similar units and summarize the findings to all three interviews in terms of the headings provided in Appendix A (e.g.," The Person and His/Her Job . . .").

3

Assessing Individual and Group Behavior

A model is provided to guide the assessment of individual and group behavior that can affect organizational effectiveness. Individual, group, and organizational forces shaping behavior are considered. Among the organizational forces examined are human resource management programs, which are designed to shape organizational behavior. Techniques for gathering, analyzing, and feeding back data on individual and group behavior are also discussed. Special attention is given to the use of standardized questionnaires.

"We need to improve service quality while cutting our costs."

"We are losing top staff people, but the less promising ones stay on."

"Our weekly program-review meetings have deteriorated to the point where we argue repeatedly about the same issues and never get anywhere."

"We need to know whether our staff development programs are producing managers who can lead our firm's expansion into the global marketplace."

The first three of these statements illustrate typical problems and challenges that clients present to behavioral science consultants. All three concern the possible effects of individual or group behavior on organizational effectiveness. The fourth statement asks for an assessment of whether a human resource management program is building staff skills that fit the organization's overall strategy.

A MODEL FOR DIAGNOSING INDIVIDUAL AND GROUP BEHAVIOR

Many forces in and around organizations can shape patterns of organizational behavior like those illustrated above. Figure 3.1 summarizes a guiding model of the important forces and outcomes to examine in diagnosis.[1] A broad diagnosis would encompass the whole range of factors shown in the figure. A focused diagnosis would consider the subsets that were found important during scouting or that most closely reflected client concerns.

The arrow in the figure that shows human resource inputs at the individual level refers to characteristics and traits employees have acquired in the past. The two boxes in the center depict the main forms of organizational behavior that shape group and individual outcomes. The outcomes shown in the figure include organizational outputs—such as products and services—group and individual performance, and quality of work life (QWL). QWL refers to the degree to which work contributes to the employees' material and psychological well-being (Nadler & Lawler, 1983; Walton, 1975). As the figure shows, lower level forces such as individual behavior can affect higher level phenomena, such as group processes and culture as well as being influenced by them. For simplicity, the model does not distinguish between divisional and organization-level phenomena, but this distinction may be important if divisions differ substantially from one another. The broken lines around the components in Figure 3.1 show their openness to environmental influences such as government regulation, labor market conditions, and societal norms. Let us look briefly at each of the major components of the model.

Outcomes

Group Performance

To assess group functioning in terms of outputs, consultants need to define the most important goods or services produced by the group and to measure their quality and quantity over a given time period. To assess quantitative outputs among units within state employment security offices, one researcher (Gresov, 1989, p. 441) counted claims processed by intake and processing units, job-seekers placed by placement units, and people counseled by employment counseling units. The outputs for administrative and professional groups with complex tasks are often hard to measure. They include solutions to problems (e.g., how to increase market share), plans (e.g., plans for AIDS education in the schools), tactics, and procedures for coordinating the work of other units.

---

1. Figure 3.1 and the following discussion draw in part on Lawler, Nadler,and Mirvis (1983, pp. 20-25) but expand that discussion considerably. Readers who are unfamiliar with the fields of organizational behavior and human resource management should consult recent texts in these fields (e.g., Gordon, 1991; Heneman, Schwab, Fossum, & Dyer, 1989) and the references cited in this chapter before conducting a diagnosis.

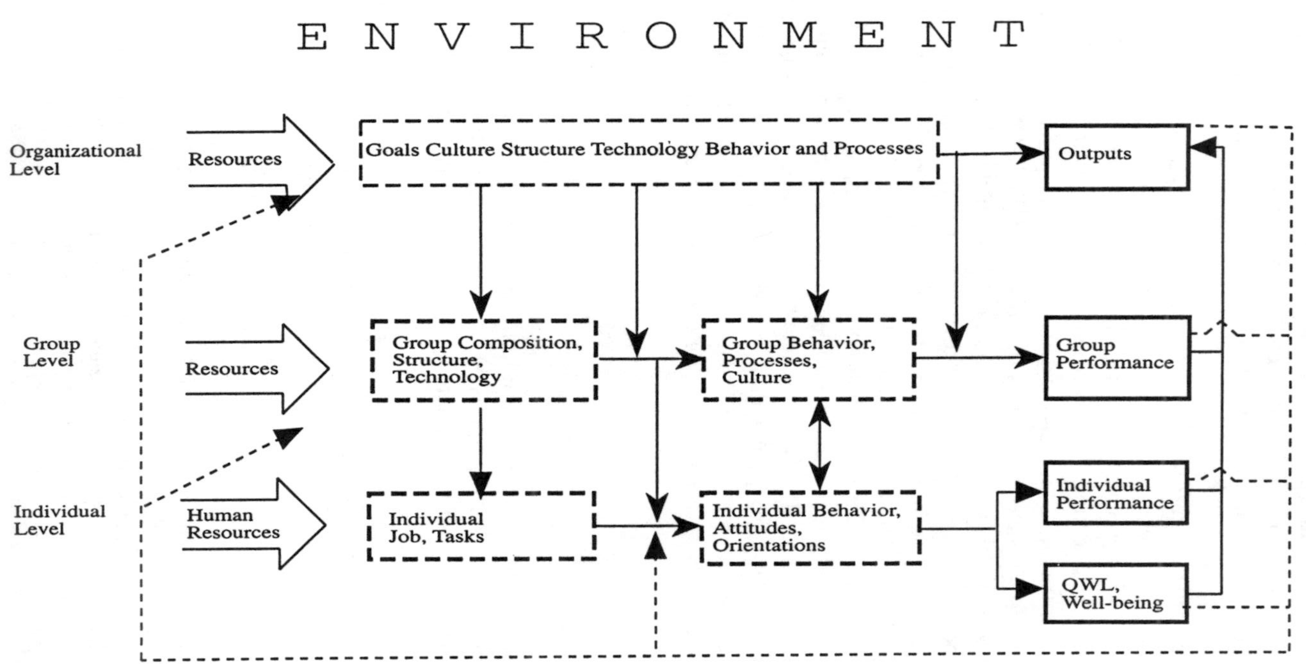

Figure 3.1. A Model for Diagnosing Individual and Group Behavior
Key: Solid lines show main lines of influence. Dotted lines show feedback loops.

Individual Performance

This category includes the degree and quality of members' efforts, their degree of initiative, cooperation with other employees, levels of absenteeism, lateness, and commitment to the job. The critical aspects of individual and group performance depend on the group's main tasks, goals, and standards. In a surveyor's team within a city agency, for example, accuracy and reliability may be more critical facets of effectiveness than speed.

Quality of Work Life (QWL) and Well-Being

Diagnostic studies often assess the employees' psychological and material well-being in terms of employees' levels of satisfaction with these conditions:

- job security
- fairness and adequacy of pay
- working conditions
- interpersonal relations
- meaningfulness and challenge of work

Investigators can obtain descriptions of working conditions from employees or rate QWL and other working conditions on the basis of observation or the judgments of experts. Diagnosis can also use objective and subjective indicators of individual health and well-being. These include rates of job-related illness, accidents, substance abuse on or off the job, and stress (Cook, Hepworth, Wall, & Wair, 1981, pp. 98-112; Ironson, 1992; Kets de Vries, 1979; Sandman, 1992).

Research shows that QWL, as indicated by satisfaction with rewards, often reduces turnover and other indicators of desire for withdrawal from the job (Fisher & Locke, 1992). Under certain conditions, improvements in QWL and employee well-being can also lead to cost savings and higher productivity (Katz, Kochan, & Weber, 1985; Walton, 1975). Even when such bottom-line results cannot be expected, managers, unions, and organizational consultants may still define improvement in QWL and well-being as desirable ends in themselves (e.g., *Business Week,* 1981; Davis & Cherns, 1975).

Factors Affecting Individual and Group Outcomes

Tables 3.1 and 3.2 summarize individual and group factors that can affect job performance, QWL, and well-being. A wide range of conditions may alter the effects of these factors. Hence, whenever possible

Table 3.1
Key Individual Factors

Human Resource Inputs (Individual Characteristics)

Physical and mental state—health, abilities, job-related traits (e.g., motor coordination, public speaking skills).
Social background and traits—sex, age; ethnic, regional, cultural background.
Training and education—formal education, technical training, work experience.
Personal values, norms, beliefs, assumptions, attitudes
Individual needs—importance of various types of rewards, job characteristics.

Job Characteristics

Pay and benefits
Meaningfulness—task identity, variety, significance (Hackman & Oldham, 1980).
Routineness
Accountability—employee is responsible for important results.
Feedback—employee gets feedback on work, sees results.
Clarity/ambiguity of responsibilities and assignments; conflict among others' expectations toward role occupant
Physical/psychological stress
Job security

Individual Orientations

Motivation—to work well, remain on job
Rewards experienced:

- Extrinsic: Pay, benefits, security, promotion prospects, peer approval, social status, nonmonetary compensation (e.g., flexible hours, training opportunities), physical conditions, location
- Intrinsic: Job felt to be interesting, challenging; personal growth, learning, feeling of accomplishment

Expectations:

- Link between performance and valued rewards (e.g., Promotion depends on good work.)
- Consequences of effort, initiative, innovation (e.g., What happens to people who find new ways of doing things?)
- Ability to get things done

Equity—feeling that efforts are fairly rewarded compared to others in organization and to other organizations.
Trust—perceived ability to rely on peers and managers and to believe in them.
Specific attitudes—satisfaction with administrative procedures (e.g., grievance mechanisms); attitudes toward and assessment of current and proposed projects, changes.

---

practitioners should directly investigate the causal impacts of the factors listed in the tables, rather than assume that these effects are universal.

Individual Factors

The individual characteristics listed in Table 3.1 can directly shape people's motivation to perform a task and their ability to do so. These human resource inputs become particularly important for organizational diagnosis when they are shared by sizable groups of employees. For example, the rise in educational levels among blue-collar workers throughout Europe and North America led workers to prefer more interesting and challenging work. Despite the influence of such human resource inputs, practitioners and clients should not overestimate their importance. It is sometimes tempting to assume that the problems of a failing program or department could be solved, if only the "right person" could be found to run it or the right staff members were chosen. When a unit's problems seem likely to persist even if the "ideal" manager and staff are found, group and organizational sources of the problem should also be investigated. Practitioners should also consider group and organizational factors when clients cannot readily alter individual factors and human resource inputs—for example, when tenured civil servants cannot be replaced or retrained.

The job characteristics listed in Table 3.1 can sometimes affect intrinsic motivation, which may affect performance (Hackman & Oldham, 1980). The redesign of jobs to allow greater challenge and group autonomy appears to contribute to work quality while reducing costs (e.g., Eisenhardt & Westcott, 1988; Florida & Kenney, 1991; Griffen, 1991). But plants that introduce job redesign usually make other structural changes as well. Improvements in performance that follow job redesign may therefore reflect structural changes unrelated to intrinsic motivation, such as increased responsibility and accountability for autonomous employees.

The third part of Table 3.1 lists individual orientations—attitudes, beliefs, and motivational states—that can also affect QWL and performance (Cranny, Smith, & Stone, 1992; Goodman, 1977; Lawler, 1977). By examining employees' expectations and understandings of their work situation, consultants may discover explanations for suboptimal performance. If people expect their efforts to go unrewarded or to yield rewards that are not important to them (e.g., citation in the company newsletter), they will remain unmotivated to work toward improvement.

Diagnoses can also benefit from the assessment of specific attitudes and perceptions about questions being debated within an organization. Consultants might, for example, ask members of an organization how they feel about specific proposals and policies, such as a voluntary

Table 3.2
Key Group Factors

Group Composition, Structure, and Technology

Social and Occupational Composition—Mix of members' characteristics (e.g., Americans versus locals in overseas office); proportions of minorities, genders; divergences of professional training and work experience (e.g., veteran managers versus new MBAs).

Structure—nature, extent of rules, types of work/decision procedures (e.g., judgment, precedent, standard operating procedures); flexibility of task assignments; control procedures (reports, supervision, computer monitoring, peer evaluation); frequency, comprehensiveness of controls (Are all processes or outcomes checked or just some?), coordination mechanisms.

Technology—impacts on group processes (e.g., noise prevents conversation; office layout encourages contact); workflow interdependencies.

Group Behavior, Processes, and Culture

Relations among group members—cohesiveness (attachment to group, similarity of views, behavior).

Processes:

- Rewarding: types of behavior rewarded (e.g., conformity vs. individuality), frequency, consistency, process of delivering rewards.
- Communication: direction of flows (up, down, across department lines), openness and honesty (Do members share problems or try to look good?).
- Cooperation and conflict—sources, extent, nature, conflict management (collaboration in search of mutually satisfactory solutions, bargaining, forcing solution by superior).
- Decision making (methods, degree of participation) and problem solving (methods, confrontation, avoidance).

Supervisory Behavior—supportiveness (encourages learning, provides help, resources); level of participation (shares information and decision making); task emphasis (stresses goal achievement, common purposes); level and nature of performance expectations (e.g., effort, quality expected); style of communication and conflict management.

Culture—group identity (language, symbols, rituals); consensus, clarity about goals, values, norms; trust, confidence in peers, managers; beliefs about work and rewards (e.g., getting ahead, risk taking); views on nature of environment, problems, challenges; fit/gap between group norms, beliefs, values and those of management.

program for early retirement. Repeated attitude surveys can also provide feedback on particular programs or groups. This information can contribute to the assessment of progress toward a stated goal and can help managers spot problems before they become critical (e.g., Nadler, Mirvis, & Cammann, 1976).

Group Factors

Table 3.2 directs attention to group-level factors that can shape individual behavior and influence outcomes at the individual, group, and organizational levels. For example, a group's social and demographic homogeneity can affect its cohesion and performance (Coombs, 1992). Moreover, the proportions of women and minorities within a group affect the pressures that these participants feel toward conformity or overachievement (Kanter, 1977).

Diagnostic studies often trace ineffective behavior to structural and technological factors such as those listed in Table 3.2. Controls for monitoring performance and evaluative standards sometimes encourage behavior that management considers undesirable, while discouraging other, desired forms of behavior (e.g., Case 8; Lawler & Rhode, 1976; Schneier, Shaw, & Beatty, 1992). For example, a supplier of products to hospitals measured the number of visits per week that each sales representative made to doctors and administrators who might order the firm's products. This indicator of performance was used as a basis for bonuses, because complicated ordering procedures within the hospital systems made it impossible for the supplier to assess directly how much its representatives contributed to sales. Monitoring and rewarding the quantity of visits encouraged sales personnel to visit the customers who were easy to locate and led them to neglect hard-to-contact administrators, who had the most influence over decisions to order the firm's products.

Many of the factors listed in the second part of Table 3.2 were treated as major determinants of group and organizational effectiveness by traditional organization development consultants (e.g., Beckhard, 1969; Schein, 1969) and adherents of the human relations model of group processes (e.g., Likert, 1967; McGregor, 1960). According to these researchers and consultants, group and organizational performance and motivation are enhanced when work groups are cooperative and cohesive, communication is honest and multidirectional, group norms support productivity, decision making is participative, and supervision is both task oriented and supportive of individual effort and learning. Recent work on transformational leadership (Bass & Avolio, 1990; Sashkin & Burke, 1990; Tichy & DeVanna, 1986) also points to the possibility that managers can enhance their effectiveness and in some cases may contribute to organizational effectiveness by inspiring subordinates to pursue group or organizational goals, stimulating them intellectually, and helping them achieve higher levels of development and maturity. The transformational leadership style contrasts with the transactional style that emphasizes management by exception and the provision of rewards in exchange for performance.

Moving groups toward the supervisory and communication styles favored by human relations and organization development does not always enhance productivity, but it usually improves work satisfaction, QWL, and job commitment (G. Strauss, 1977, 1982). Moreover, employee involvement in quality circles and other forms of participative decision making can enhance work quality and facilitate creativity and innovation (Lawler, 1986). However, the benefits of such participative innovations may disappear after a few years (Griffen, 1988). Moreover, participative innovations such as quality circles cannot overcome the effects of polarized labor relations and may add little to organizations that already enjoy cooperative labor-management relations (Katz, Kochan, & Weber, 1985). Both labor and middle management may resist implementation of quality circles and other participative programs because they view the programs as a threat to their power or job security. Practitioners should, therefore, consider carefully the potential costs of such innovations and the barriers to their implementation before recommending them to clients (Lawler, 1986; Shea, 1986).

Organizational Factors

Diagnostic studies can profitably explore the effects on individual and group outcomes of the entire range of organizational factors appearing in the top level of Figure 3.1. For instance, patterns of individual and group performance can often be traced to organizational strategies, standards, and goals, all of which help shape the targets that lower level managers use to evaluate performance. Group norms often reflect the employees' sense of how best to achieve the performance targets that have become established throughout the organization. Thus when a department chair tells staff members "We're a publish or perish university," faculty members translate that into a simple injunction: "Forget about preparing classes and meeting with students. Concentrate on your research!"

The level of trust between ranks and functions can also affect individual and group behavior (Fox, 1974). Trust can affect people's identification with organizational objectives, compliance with administrative procedures, and willingness to negotiate mutually acceptable resolutions to disagreements and conflicts. Employees who place more trust in their managers may also be more willing to accept the changes their managers propose (Smith, 1992).

Organizational technology and structure shape coordination and control within groups; the division of labor within and between groups; and the nature of individual-level tasks. Organizational culture can shape the beliefs and assumptions that focus people's attention and channel their efforts. Chief among these are beliefs about the way work gets done, how change occurs, who is powerful, what clients and customers expect, and how external trends and developments affect the organization (Argyris & Schon, 1978; Davis, 1984; Kotter & Heskett, 1992; Schein, 1985; Starbuck, Greve, & Hedberg, 1978).

Organizational Factors: Human Resource Management Programs

In addition to the broad types of organizational factors discussed above, diagnosis of individual and group behavior can examine the impacts of official human resource management (HRM) activities. These are programs and actions that are explicitly intended to shape the skills, knowledge, attitudes, and behavior of employees. A broad assessment of HRM impacts would encompass all HRM activities that may directly shape organizational behavior (Heneman et al., 1989), including:

- external staffing (recruitment, selection)
- internal staffing (placement, promotion, discharge, retirement)
- development (on- and off-the-job training, career planning)
- compensation (pay and benefits)
- labor relations (contract negotiation and administration, grievances, employee rights)
- work environment (job design, occupational health and safety)

The following supporting HRM operations would also be investigated:

- goal setting
- planning (linking HRM to organizational strategy and goals; forecasting trends and planning actions)
- job analysis (skill requirements, rewards, motivational potential)
- evaluation and performance assessment

More problem-oriented and focused diagnoses could treat one or more of these HRM areas as the main object for investigation. Case 7, for instance, presents an illustration of how a consultant might diagnose management training and development programs within a firm moving toward transnational operations—a complex, decentralized set of operations in many countries with many strategic alliances to local firms:[2]

Case 7

To start, the practitioner would define the skills needed for managing a truly transnational firm. Among these skills are the ability to interact simultaneously with people from many cultures, to learn from them, and to treat them as equals. The practitioner would examine whether training programs, on-the-job experiences, and career development among the firm's managers are likely to foster these skills. To assess the impacts of training programs, for example, the practitioner could check whether curriculum and instructional techniques are designed to promote the needed skills. If so, the practitioner could directly measure the outcomes of training to see whether these formal objectives are achieved in practice. Recommendations would focus on closing the gap between current and desired practices to enhance skill development. Management might, for example, increase multinational participation in training programs and treat international experience and cultural adaptability as important criteria for career development and promotion.

DIAGNOSTIC METHODS AND PROCEDURES

The section that follows examines the design and administration of a diagnosis of the forces affecting individual and group outcomes. It also notes general issues that arise in most diagnoses, no matter what questions or organizational levels are emphasized.

Study Design

Deciding What to Study

Consultants usually select topics for study in response to their clients' initial presentations of problems, in keeping with the preliminary diag-

---

2. Derived from a report by Adler and Bartholomew (1992) of a study of the human resource programs in 50 North American firms. The study assessed the degree to which these programs contribute to the development of the competencies required for managers in transnational firms.

nosis made during scouting. For instance, the complaint about the argument-ridden, unproductive meetings cited at the beginning of the chapter might lead a consultant to explore the background to the arguments that plague the meetings. Preliminary conversations with participants might reveal major disagreements about program goals along with a lack of mechanisms for working out such difficulties. In keeping with these findings the consultant could explore goal-setting and decision-making processes more closely.

The choice of diagnostic topics also reflects the effectiveness criteria to be used in assessing individual and group behavior. In addition to the individual and group outcomes discussed in this chapter, many of the system-state criteria listed in Table 2.1 and developed in Table 3.2 can also serve as standards for evaluating work groups. Rancorous conflict, for example, can be treated as a sign of group ineffectiveness. Practitioners can also apply the adaptation and resource-position criteria in Table 2.1 to small groups by defining the group's environment as including other units within the focal organization, along with parts of the organization's environment.

Having chosen a particular focus for diagnosis, the practitioner must define carefully the specific factors to be studied and decide on the best ways to obtain data on them. To start, practitioners can gather Basic Organizational Information and conduct a limited number of General Orientation Interviews. They can design additional data-gathering steps as needed. For example, a consultant seeking to examine conflict management and problem solving could interview group members, paying particular attention to the kinds of issues that create conflicts and the ways that members and supervisors deal with these conflicts. These data might then be supplemented with observations of group meetings (see Appendix C).

Studies that focus on assessing particular HRM programs can compare data on actual practices to criteria derived from a goal statement or ideal standard (e.g., Case 7). Sometimes a quasi-experimental design (Cook, Campbell, & Peracchio, 1991) may be used in HRM assessment (e.g., Eden, 1986). Suppose that the human resources unit of a large trucking firm sought to assess the effectiveness of a safety program that would give cash bonuses to safe drivers. If the investigators could arrange to have drivers randomly assigned to the new program, they could compare the accident and traffic violation records of program participants before and after participation in the program. These results would be compared to those of the nonparticipants over the same period. Follow-up would be necessary to determine whether these effects eroded over time. This outcome often occurs in demonstration projects and training programs.

Sampling

The data should be as representative as possible of the individuals, groups, and situations under study. For example, to find out about the characteristic ways in which conflicts are handled, the practitioner should look for typical or representative conflict episodes as well as ensuring that a cross-section of group members is interviewed. To reach large numbers of people, self-administered questionnaires can be distributed to samples of members selected through probability sampling (Judd et al., 1991). Probability samples can also be used to gather secondary data, such as absenteeism rates from large data sets. Practitioners rarely use complex probability sampling techniques to choose subjects for interviewing because of the high cost of conducting a large number of interviews. When small groups are to be interviewed or given questionnaires, all members may be included or a cross-section of individuals that is likely to hold different perspectives can be selected.

In designing samples, practitioners should take into account the attitudes of group members toward the study and the uses to which the data will be put as well as strictly methodological considerations. If, for example, all members of a large division will receive feedback from a questionnaire about their departments' operations, it may be better to include everyone in the survey. By doing so consultants may increase interest in the questionnaire study and enhance the believability of the feedback.

Data gathering through observation also raises sampling issues. Since large-scale observation is expensive and time consuming, consultants usually prefer to observe important meetings, training sessions, or crucial work activities in which members interact intensively and many aspects of group relations can be seen at the same time (see Appendix C). It is best to choose settings for observation that are as central to group operations as possible, since behavior can vary greatly from one context (e.g., headquarters) to another (e.g., field operations). Practitioners should also be aware that a unit may operate differently when it convenes as a whole, than when its members work alone or in subgroups.

Administering the Study

Procedures used to gather, store, and analyze the data should promote sound relations between consultants and members of the organization as well as providing valid diagnostic data.[3] Practitioners should make it clear to members of a client organization that they will store and process the data professionally and maintain the confidentiality of participants. Moreover, they should explain that only group-level results will be reported, to preserve the anonymity of individual members.

Measurement and Data-Gathering Techniques

By using a combination of data-gathering techniques consultants can enhance the validity of their findings. The following discussion concentrates on questionnaires because of their popularity and appropriateness to the individual and group levels of analysis.

Analyzing Available Data

Practitioners can extract data on the social or personal characteristics of work group members from the personnel files of a client organization or ask to have such data prepared for them. They can use standard content-analysis procedures to analyze the data (Selltiz, Wrightsman, & Cooke, 1976). Most for-profit organizations and a growing proportion of not-for-profits also have records of group outputs such as sales, productivity, product quality (e.g., percentage of products serviced under warranty), and services delivered (e.g., number of outpatient visits to a hospital clinic). Organizational publications and records may also provide information on processes, structures, technologies, and purposes, but such information will be hard to code and quantify. Documentary data almost always need to be supplemented with information on actual practices (chapter 4).

Organizational documents or records frequently reflect the perspectives of those who gathered the information and the reasons for which it was originally gathered. Employee evaluations used to make decisions about pay raises, for example, may reflect the pressures that immediate supervisors felt to present their subordinates in a favorable light. In contrast, negative comments about these employees by more senior managers may reflect a desire to avoid granting raises automatically. By examining both sets of views, the practitioner can better understand the ways that members of the focal organization interpret employee behavior and the factors shaping their interpretations. But the practitioner cannot accept either set of evaluations as unbiased.

---

3. See Bowditch and Buono (1989) and Nadler (1977) for excellent guides to conducting diagnostic surveys; Tyson et al. (1988) also discuss the uses of organizational surveys.

Interviews

Interviews can include relevant questions from the General Orientation Interview or focus on selected human resource programs and group and individual outcomes and behavior patterns. Department heads may provide basic information on their departments and work groups, but they may be reluctant to report candidly on processes and behavior that may reflect badly upon their own performance. In such cases, interviews will be needed with other department members.

By conducting detailed interviews with members from different backgrounds and locations within a unit and by listening carefully to their accounts of important issues, investigators can become aware of members' distinct perspectives and viewpoints. For example, department heads might characterize their organization as dealing honestly and directly with employee grievances, while subordinates complain that their grievances are ignored or minimized by management. The people interviewed may be unaware of such a diversity of viewpoints or intolerant of the feelings and perceptions of others. In such cases consultants can summarize the various viewpoints during feedback to stimulate communication and encourage people to respect diverse perspectives and opinions. In other instances consultants can simply take note of divergent viewpoints, to avoid giving undue weight to one particular interpretation when formulating their own descriptions and analyses.

Interviews and questionnaire studies are often subject to bias because respondents seek to present themselves in a favorable light or withhold information, such as negative descriptions of supervisors, that they fear may be used against them. Practitioners can help overcome these concerns by gradually building relations of trust with group members.

Practitioners are sometimes able to develop such relations with one or more members of an organization who know a lot about organizational affairs but are somewhat detached from them.[4] Assistants to high-level managers, for example, often have a comprehensive view of their organization and may be more comfortable describing it than the top managers are. When such well-placed individuals trust consultants, they may provide useful information about sensitive subjects, such as the degree of influence of managers who officially have the same level of authority, or staff members' past reactions to risk-taking behavior. Gathering such sensitive information poses tricky ethical issues, several of which are discussed in chapter 6.

4. In anthropological studies, such individuals are called informants, a term that cannot be used in diagnosis because of its negative connotations.

Self-Administered Questionnaires

Self-administered questionnaires offer the least expensive way of eliciting attitudes, perceptions, beliefs, and reports of behavior from a large number of individuals. Aggregations of individual responses can also provide a substitute for behavioral measures of group and organizational phenomena. Although questionnaires typically use fixed-choice answers, a few open-ended questions can be included to give respondents an opportunity to express themselves. Responses to such open-ended questions are often informative but difficult to code. Questionnaires composed of items drawn from previous research studies and from standardized organizational surveys (Appendix B) can be prepared and administered rapidly, since there is less need to develop and pretest the instrument. By including standard measures consultants may also be able to compare the responses obtained in the client organization with results from other organizations in which the same instrument was used.

Standardized Instruments

One of the most useful and comprehensive standardized instruments is the Michigan Organizational Assessment Questionnaire (MOAQ) (Cammann, Fichman, Jenkins, et al., 1983; Appendix B), which is part of a battery of instruments in the Michigan Quality of Work Program (Seashore, Lawler, Mirvis, & Cammann, 1983). MOAQ includes seven modules that cover individual performance and QWL outcomes and most of the individual factors listed in Table 3.1. MOAQ modules also cover many of the group processes and beliefs listed in Table 3.2.

To create a comprehensive diagnostic instrument, practitioners can supplement the data from MOAQ with more behavioral data on individual and group outputs and can gather additional data on the group processes, structures, technology, and external relations listed in Table 3.2. The Organizational Assessment Inventory (OAI) (Van de Ven & Ferry, 1980; Appendix B) provides many scales in these areas as well as group outcome measures and many items that overlap with MOAQ. OAI contains separate questionnaires for supervisors and group members so that comparisons of their attitudes and reports can be made. Other instruments within OAI assess divisional (interdepartmental) and organization-level phenomena.

To obtain data on group-level phenomena from questionnaires such as MOAQ and OAI, the responses from members of a particular work group or administrative unit are averaged to create group scores. For these averages to be meaningful, the questionnaires must specify clearly which work groups and supervisors are referred to. Otherwise the data cannot be used to diagnose the operations of specific groups or to provide feedback to group managers and members.

Advantages and Drawbacks of Standardized Questionnaires

MOAQ and OAI are diagnostic tools that are extensively documented and validated and reflect current research. Unlike earlier instruments (e.g., Blake & Mouton, 1964; Taylor & Bowers, 1972), that were based on models that advocated a single administrative style, these newer assessment packages reflect the widely accepted view that there is no one best way to organize groups or organizations. Instead, the optimal combination of system traits is assumed to depend on many variables including the environment, tasks, technology, personnel, history, and size of the organization.

Despite their obvious appeal, standardized diagnostic instruments also have serious weaknesses and drawbacks. First, they may give practitioners a false sense of confidence that all the factors relevant to a particular client organization have been covered adequately. Second, since standard questions are necessarily abstract, they may not be fully applicable to a particular organization or situation. For example, a typical questionnaire item in MOAQ asks respondents to indicate their degree of agreement with the statement, "My supervisor encourages subordinates to participate in making important decisions" (Cammann et al., 1983, p. 108). But the responses to this general statement may mask the fact that the supervisor encourages participation in decisions in one area, such as work scheduling, while making decisions alone in other areas, such as budgeting. To obtain data on such situational variations, investigators must determine the situations across which there may be broad variations and write questions about these situations (e.g., Enz, 1989; Moch, Cammann, & Cooke, 1983, pp. 199-200).

Third, as in any questionnaire, even apparently simple questions may contain concepts or phrases that may be understood in different ways. For instance, when reacting to the statement, "I get to do a number of different things on my job" (Cammann et al., 1983, p. 94), one person might see diversity in physical actions (e.g., snipping versus scraping) or minor changes in the tools needed for the job, whereas another would consider all of those operations as "doing the same thing." Fourth, questionnaires are especially vulnerable to biases stemming from the respondent's desire to give socially acceptable answers or to avoid sensitive issues. There may also be tendencies to give artificially consistent responses (Salancik & Pfeffer, 1977; but compare Stone, 1992). Some instruments include questions designed to detect or minimize biases, whereas others may heighten bias by phrasing all questions in a single direction.

Observations

Observations can help consultants get a firsthand feel for the actual behavior and processes that occur within an organization and for the ways that members view their work and the organization as a whole. Direct observation can also provide practitioners with data that is more independent of the members' interpretations and viewpoint than are responses to questionnaires and interviews. People are often not very good observers of the actions occurring within their groups. Often they cannot describe group norms, beliefs, and informal behavior patterns or are reluctant to do so. Since observation is time consuming and requires keen skills, it is often reserved for the analysis of top management groups, whose decisions and solutions to problems are critical to the organization as a whole.

Meetings make an ideal focus for observations. Managers and professionals spend much of their time in meetings, and meeting outcomes form an important part of managerial outputs. Moreover, participants often find meetings to be frustrating and nonproductive. Hence they may be interested in having consultants help them improve the effectiveness of their meetings.

Observational Techniques

Consultants can structure observations in terms of a general accounting scheme (Appendix C; Perkins, Nadler, & Hanlon, 1981) or predefined categories for coding observed behavior (Weick, 1985). Experienced practitioners may also conduct unstructured observations to remain open to unanticipated phenomena.

Unless observers use a highly structured coding scheme, they briefly record the observed behavior of the participants using descriptive, nonevaluative language—for example:

> "Chairperson shouts for order."
>
> "Workers consult each other over how to get the machine going again."
>
> "Nurses are quiet, do not participate in the discussion of the case."

Notations on observed behavior such as these provide data on which subsequent inferences about group functioning are based. For example, repeated observations of workers helping each other handle snags in operations may lead consultants to conclude that relations between workers are cooperative and facilitate independence from supervisors and technicians. Including such concrete descriptions of behavior will also make feedback more useful to group members. If the practitioners have used a list of topics to guide their observations, they can summarize their findings for each topic and add illustrative descriptions from their notes.

Before beginning observations of a particular setting, investigators often try to learn as much as possible through interviews or informal conversations about the backgrounds of the people to be observed, their roles, the nature of the task facing the group, and the ways that this task or similar ones have been handled in the past. If taking notes during the observations will disturb group members, observers should record their notes as soon as possible after the observation. With practice, observers can recall entire conversations or discussions and record them after completing the observation. Things which the observer did not understand can be clarified through repeated observations or discussions with participants. Additional observations of the group under differing circumstances and repeated observations of similar events will help the observer distinguish between recurring and one-time phenomena. Once a clear picture has emerged, results can be compared to those obtained from other data sources and prepared for analysis and feedback.

Analysis

Analysis of diagnostic data can draw on the logical and statistical procedures used in nonapplied research (Judd et al., 1991; A. Strauss, 1987). Once summarized, nonstatistical data can be analyzed with the help of diagrams such as Figure 3.1. The main findings about each of the categories shown could be recorded on an enlarged version of the figure. The arrows between the boxes in the figure could be labeled to describe important system interactions. For example, the figure might display a link between the tasks of clerical workers (limited authority and access to information) and their job orientations (boredom, alienation). Beneath the figure supporting evidence of the relation could be recorded—such as the observation that clerical employees who were given more responsibility and information showed higher motivation and less boredom.

If the study includes standard, quantifiable measures on which data exist for other organizations, consultants can compare the findings for the client organization with these baseline data. More frequently, practitioners make statistical or qualitative comparisons among all similar units (e.g., departments or work teams) within the organization on all of the effectiveness measures and on variables that are assumed to lead to effectiveness. They isolate for further study groups that are unusually high or low on the measures or prepare the data for feedback to group members. Alternatively, if previous investigations suggested that certain units were outstanding or problematic in some important feature, such as in quality of service or innovativeness, consultants may concentrate on examining the characteristics of these units.

Before undertaking extended multivariate analyses of questionnaire data, practitioners should decide how heavily their diagnosis will rely on these analyses. Alternatively, they could use other methods to gather additional information or provide members of the client group with the major single or bivariate distributions and encourage them to try to account for the findings from their understandings of the organization. Whatever approach is chosen, the data should be presented in an appealing and easy-to-understand form. Reports and trade literature that circulate in a client organization may demonstrate appropriate formats for presenting data.

Feedback

Procedures

Wide variations exist in procedures for providing feedback from diagnostic studies (Nadler, 1977). Practitioners may only give feedback to the client or clients who called for the study. More frequently, where feedback encourages group problem solving, consultants present their results to all participants in the study or to everyone affected by its findings. Consultants can give feedback to supervisors and members of an organizational unit separately or simultaneously. The major danger in providing feedback simultaneously to supervisors and subordinates is that supervisors often experience conflicts between receiving criticism and being expected to lead a discussion about planning appropriate action. An alternative design involves providing feedback to task forces or other temporary groups that cut across departmental and hierarchical lines. These groups are assigned responsibility for planning the organization's response to the findings.

In client-focused diagnoses in organization development consultations, consultants usually try to collaborate with members of the client organization to interpret the findings and decide how to deal with them (Burke, 1982, p. 162). To start, the consultant presents a summary of the data and a preliminary analysis. A discussion usually follows in which consultant and participants clarify the findings. Then the practitioner and group members discuss the implications of the data for action.

Feedback Characteristics

Whatever form feedback takes, people are more likely to accept and act upon it when the feedback is (Block, 1981; Cummings & Huse, 1989, pp. 102-104):

1. Relevant and understandable to members.
2. Descriptive, rather than evaluative.
3. Clear and specific—referring to concrete behavior and situations, illustrating generalizations.
4. Comparative—including comparisons to similar units or organizations.
5. Timely—given shortly after data gathering.
6. Believable—providing information about the validity of the data.
7. Sensitive to members' feelings and motivations—rather than provoking anger, defensiveness, or feelings of helplessness.
8. Limited, rather than overwhelming.
9. Practical and feasible—pointing to issues that members can do something about.
10. Unfinalized—leaving room for members to make their own interpretations and decisions about action.

Even if practitioners cannot meet these exacting standards completely, they can improve their effectiveness by moving their feedback procedures closer to these ideals.

EXERCISES

1. Using Questionnaires to Diagnose Group Processes

Choose two work groups or units on which background information is available. These groups should perform similar tasks and have similar types of employees. Try to locate one group reputed to have positive features (e.g., high work quality or positive staff relations) and another that seems weak in the same areas. Develop a questionnaire on key aspects of group process with about 10 questions drawn from one or more of the standardized questionnaires discussed in this chapter and Appendix B. Distribute the questionnaire to members of both groups after you have explained that the data will be used only for an exercise and will not be distributed to anyone outside of the groups. Prepare a summary of the average responses to each question for two groups and compare your results to the previous information you had on the groups. If the results differ from your expectations, try to account for these differences. Explain how you would give feedback to the supervisors and members of both groups to facilitate constructive discussion and problem solving. If requested, prepare a separate summary of the findings for each group.

2. Observing Meetings

Choose features of group behavior, processes, and culture listed in Table 3.2 or in Appendix C that can be observed during group meetings. Observe at least two meetings of the same group. Write a report on the following topics:

1. Background on the group and the meetings (type of meetings, purpose, circumstances—e.g., weekly staff meetings, emergency session, etc.—participants, organizational context, etc.).
2. Summary of observations of the selected group features.
3. Criteria for evaluating group effectiveness.
4. Sources of effectiveness and ineffectiveness.
5. Possible ways to improve effectiveness.
6. Procedure for providing feedback to participants.

3. Assessing Human Resource Management Programs

Choose one HRM function—for example, staff development—from the lists in this chapter. Interview the manager who has the most direct responsibility for administering operations in this area, for example, the director of personnel. Ask this person to define the organization's needs and activities in this functional area in terms of the desired individual and group characteristics or outcomes. Ask what standards are currently used to assess whether these needs are being met and whether any internal or external developments require redefinitions of these needs and standards. Based on this interview, write a proposal to diagnose the extent to which current HRM programs, such as on-the-job-training, meet current and anticipated needs. Be specific about the units of analysis, the kinds of data to be gathered, and the types of inferences you will make from these data.

4

System Fits and Power Relations

The open system model is used as a guide for assessing the fit between such elements as structure, environment, technology, and goals. Emphasis is placed on aspects of organization design that managers can influence. Fits between actual behavior and official objectives and practices are also discussed. The final section of the chapter treats ways to assess the distribution and uses of power—one of the most critical features of actual behavior.

This chapter shows how to use the system model to uncover conditions that shape the effectiveness of entire divisions or the organization as a whole. These *macro-level conditions* become critical when major changes occur in key system elements, such as the environment, or in technology. Divisional or organization-wide forces may contribute to problems such as:

- Poor-quality or customer/client relations
- Stagnant or falling sales and revenues
- Loss of public support or confidence
- Failure to keep up with competitors and industrial or sectoral standards
- Bitter, enduring conflicts between units
- Tasks being neglected or falling between the cracks
- Lack of innovation or creativity
- Inability to recruit top candidates for jobs
- Failure to execute complex projects
- Unintended consequences of plans and programs
- Communication delays and failures

To diagnose the causes of problems such as these, practitioners can examine how well an organization's system elements and subcomponents fit with one another and directly assess the consequences of tight or loose fits. To assess the likely impacts of changes in one or more system elements such as technology, practitioners can examine the fit between the element undergoing change and other system features such as administrative processes.

The terms *fit, congruence,* and *alignment* refer to the extent to which the behavioral or organizational requirements and constraints in one part of a system are compatible with those in other parts (Beer, 1980; Nadler & Tushman, 1980a, 1980b; Van de Ven & Drazin, 1985).[1] In addition to creating macro-organizational problems, poor fits within divisions or within the organization as a whole can produce micro-level symptoms—those that affect individual, interpersonal, and group outcomes, such as task performance, satisfaction, and turnover. Members of a client organization who are used to dealing with problems in terms of individual motivation or interpersonal relations may not always see the connections between such symptoms and macro-level conditions.

DIAGNOSING SYSTEM FITS

The following case (Beckhard & Harris, 1975, p. 52) illustrates how poor fit between system elements at the divisional level can affect motivation and individual behavior:

Case 8

> The head of a major corporate division was frustrated by his subordinates' lack of motivation to work with him in planning for the future of the business and by their lack of attention to developing the managerial potential of their subordinates. Repeated exhortations about these matters produced few results, although the division managers agreed that change was desirable. The barrier to change was that the managers were held directly accountable for short-term profits in their divisions. There were no meaningful rewards for engaging in planning or management development and no punishments for not doing so. But if the managers failed to show a profit, they would be fired on the spot.

This case shows the effect of incongruence between some of the division's objectives and its reward and control mechanisms—components of its structure. The division's objectives included planning and management development, but its reward and control procedures failed

1. It is also possible to examine fits among different system levels, for example, individual-group, individual-organization, group-organization fits (see Nadler & Tushman, 1980a).

to encourage managers to develop their subordinates and instead led them to strive exclusively for more tangible, short-term results. Misfits such as these can stem from inertia and lack of attention to achieving system congruity, bureaucratic pressures, and conflicts among the many external and internal constraints to which management is subject (Gresov, 1989).

Figure 4.1 provides a schematic summary of the steps required to diagnose fits. The first step in the figure, The Choice of Fits, is treated in the next section. The second and third steps are addressed in the sections Ways to Assess Fits, (page 86), Diagnosing Organization Design (page 87), and Actual Practices Versus Official Mandates (page 94). The fourth step is discussed in Assessing the Impacts of Fits (page 97).

The Choice of Fits

A Checklist of Important Fits

One way to choose fits for diagnosis is to start with a checklist such as the one in Table 4.1 of fits that research and consulting practice have shown to be especially important.[2] In a comprehensive diagnostic study practitioners can examine each of these fits in at least a preliminary fashion and can look for changes that are likely to disrupt current fits. Since the divisions of large, complex organizations will differ from one another in all or most of the system elements (e.g., environment, technology, structure), it is best to begin by examining fits within divisions. If necessary, fits within the total organization can be considered subsequently.

Starting With Client Problems

Consultants who prefer a more focused and practical approach can examine fits that are most directly related to the problems that clients present or that emerged during scouting. During the investigation, the practitioner branches out to look for underlying conditions related to

---

2. The following sources also treat the fits shown in Table 4.1: Porter (1980) on strategy/environment fits; Pfeffer (1981a) on goals/culture; Newman and Warren (1981) and Harrison and Phillips (1991) on goals, plans/technology, behavior; Fombrun, Tichy, and De Vanna (1984), Schuler and MacMillan (1984) on human resources/goals and strategies; Hall (1987) on structure (size)/technology; Steele (1973) on structure (physical layout)/ technology and processes; Jamieson and O'Mara (1991) on structure/human resources; Greenlagh (1986), Pondy (1967), and Walton and Dutton (1969) on official structures/ actual behavior (conflicts).

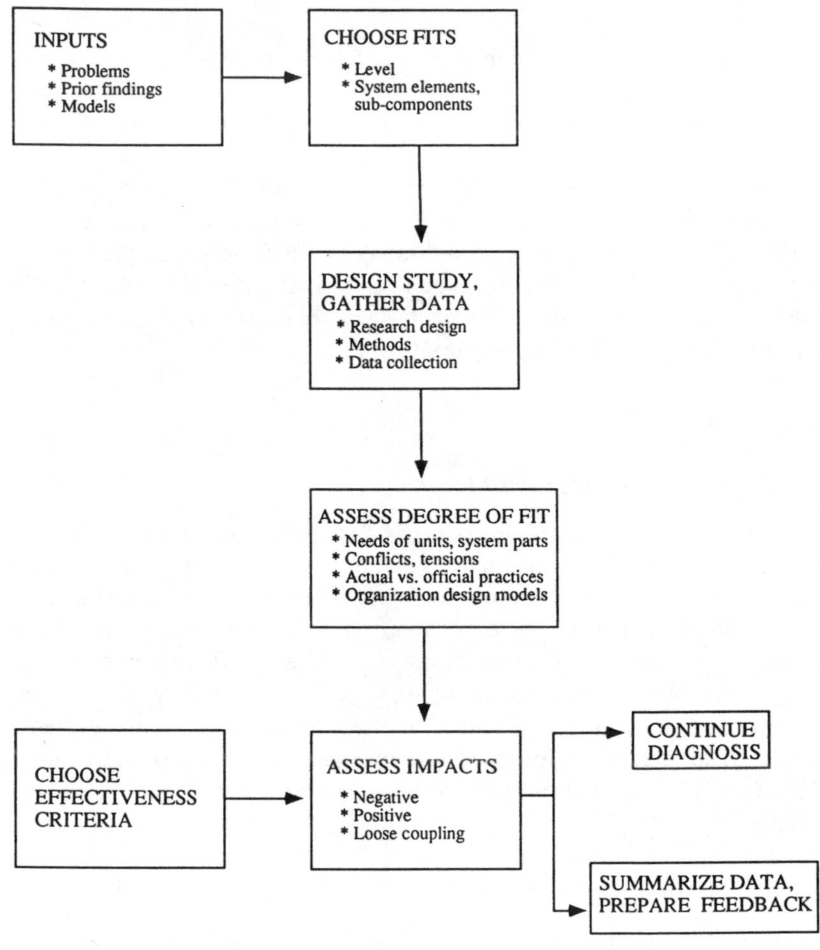

Figure 4.1. Diagnosing System Fits

the client's problems that also have a wider impact on organizational effectiveness. By discovering these underlying conditions, the practitioner can find ways to solve the presented problems and enhance overall effectiveness.

For example, the practitioner who encounters complaints about tasks being neglected or handled poorly can deal with these problems by clarifying the links between structure and two critical processes: decision

Table 4.1
Questions About Fits

Focal Area	*Does focal area fit with . . .*
Environment	*Inputs* Does the environment provide the resources needed for smooth operations, including funds, services, information, and people? Are external changes likely to change key resource flows? *Outputs* Is the demand for current products and services changing? Are external developments likely to lead to such changes? Do products and services meet the expectations of clients, customers, and other external stakeholders?
Goals and Strategies	*Environment* Do current goals, strategies, and tactics help the organization gain and maintain a favorable position in its environment? Is the organization directing its products and services to the appropriate environmental niches? Are there other unexploited markets and environments? *Resources* Can strategies and programs be supported by available resources? *Behavior, Culture* Does management create a sense of mission and identity among members and successfully project the organizational identity to external stakeholders? Are plans to introduce change compatible with current norms, values, behavior, and beliefs? *Technology, Behavior, and Processes* Do plans and objectives contribute to work processes or are they too rigid to handle unforeseen developments?
Human Resources	*Structure, Technology, Processes* Do employees' skills and training fit their job requirements and equip them to handle new tasks and technologies? Are the best people attracted and retained by the rewards and advancement opportunities offered? Are professionals and others seeking autonomy and challenge assigned to less-structured and less tightly controlled jobs? *Goals, Strategies* Do the skills, knowledge, and culture of current employees fit goals and strategies?

(Continued)

Table 4.1
Continued

Focal Area	*Does focal area fit with . . .*
Technology	*Environment* Do current technologies meet industry or sectoral standards and fulfill the expectations of suppliers, clients, and customers? *Culture* Do current and proposed technologies fit prevailing values, norms, and beliefs within the organization?
Structure, Processes, Culture	*Environment* How good is the fit between the focal organization and its partners in mergers and strategic alliances? How well do administrative practices bridge members of the organization to customers, clients, and external partners?
Structure	*Technology, Environment, Processes* Are people who must work together grouped in units or otherwise linked structurally? Are divisions or subunits large enough to handle routine tasks efficiently but small enough to adjust quickly to new environmental and technological developments? Are procedures for coordinating work and information flows appropriate to the tasks, technology, and environmental constraints? Have administrative practices been redesigned to facilitate the operation of new technical systems and take full advantage of them? Are there tasks and functions that no one does adequately and others on which people or units overlap needlessly? Are divisional (or subunit) structures differentiated enough to allow them to handle the special problems created by their particular environments, technologies, and tasks? Are the mechanisms for coordination between units adequate for the level of differentiation? Are authority and responsibility located sufficiently low in the hierarchy? Does the physical and geographic layout of the division contribute to the flow of work and information? *Human Resources* How well do work arrangements, routines, regulations, and human resource development programs meet the needs of diverse groups of employees, including older employees, those with physical disabilities, and single parents?

(Continued)

Table 4.1
Continued

Focal Area	*Does focal area fit with . . .*
Official Goals, Structures, and Processes	*Actual Behavior, Processes, Culture* Are managerial objectives and procedures supported by actual norms and processes and behavior? Do members regard official rules and procedures as fair and sensible? Do reward and control mechanisms encourage behavior and group norms that are compatible with managerial objectives? *Actual Behavior, Processes* Are group actions and decisions carried out without bitter conflicts or power struggles? Does competition among units encourage or undermine performance and support for overall goals and objectives? Do people and units have enough power and resources to accomplish their tasks adequately? Do they have the power to innovate and improve the organization?

making and communication. *Responsibility charting,* a procedure used in many large corporations (Galbraith, 1977, p. 171), provides one way to clarify these links. First, during interviews or workshops the practitioner asks group members to list key tasks or decision areas. In a project group these might include budgeting, scheduling, allocating personnel, and changing design specifications of a product. Second, each member is asked to list the positions that might be involved in these areas (e.g., project director, general manager, laboratory manager) and to indicate who is assigned responsibility for performing tasks and who is supposed to approve the work, be consulted, and be informed. The data usually reveal ambiguities relating to one or more task areas. Consultants can use these data as feedback to stimulate efforts to redefine responsibilities and clarify relations. Feedback can also lead clients and consultants to evaluate fundamental organizational features, such as the degree of delegation of authority, communication patterns, and the division of labor. For instance, discussion of approval procedures for work scheduling might reveal that many minor scheduling changes are needed and that scheduling would operate more smoothly if middle-level managers received the authority to make such minor changes and inform the project head afterward.

Fits Involving Design Tools

Consultants to management often concentrate their diagnoses on fits involving *design tools*—organizational arrangements, such as job responsibilities, which can most readily be redesigned by their clients (Beer, 1980, p. 27; Mintzberg, 1979). As Case 8 suggests, procedures for rewarding, monitoring, and evaluating performance are among the most powerful design tools. By recalculating bonus pay so that it reflected contributions to planning and management development, the division head was able to correct the problem described in the case.

Other design tools to consider during diagnosis include:

- Contractual arrangements, network ties, and strategic alliances (mergers, joint ventures) with other organizations
- Structural grouping of positions and units
- Positions and procedures that monitor the environment
- Job designs
- Human resource programs
- Management information systems
- Mechanisms for coordinating internal and external relations among units or positions
- Performance control and quality assurance procedures
- Accounting and budgeting systems
- Geographic location and physical layout
- Communication channels (including bottom-up and organization-environment communications)

Design tools can structure the options available to members and create pressures to act in a particular fashion. The greater the authority and autonomy of clients, the more readily they can make changes in these design factors and thereby shape organizational behavior. Collective bargaining agreements, government regulations, and internal opposition may severely restrict the design options available to both public and private-sector managers.

Ways to Assess Fits

One practical way to assess fits is to examine the compatibility of the requirements, needs, or procedures of different units or system parts. The fits among units are weak if the work of one unit, such as the medical staff of a hospital outpatient clinic, is disrupted because of inadequate inputs from another unit, such as the X-ray department. Incompatibility among units and system parts often shows up in divergent or conflicting messages about the kinds of behavior required. For example, reporters in a newspaper bureau were told that their job responsibilities included suggesting topics for stories. But the reporters learned from their experiences in staff meetings that it did not pay to challenge the editor's leadership in this area.

A second way to assess fit is to investigate whether participants feel subject to conflicting expectations or pressures and to check whether these conflicts are the result of lacks of fit. In Case 8, for example, a department manager might have complained during an interview, "My boss wants me to work on management development, but if I do, I'll be in hot water when he goes over my quarterly sales results!" The practitioner would then check whether other managers made similar comments and whether rewards were closely tied to quarterly performance, while ignoring management development activities.

A third possibility is to see whether system elements or components fit together in ways that organizational research suggests they should (e.g., Nightingale & Toulouse, 1977; Miles & Snow, 1978; Mintzberg, 1979; Table 4.1). The next section describes models of organization design that can help practitioners assess the fits between organizational structure and other system elements.

DIAGNOSING ORGANIZATION DESIGN

Coordinating Work and Information Flows

One helpful model specifies the ability of coordination mechanisms to handle work interdependencies (Galbraith, 1977; Tichy, 1983; Tushman & Nadler, 1978). This model distinguishes among three types of interdependencies:

Pooled interdependencies—where units can work independently of each other (e.g., crews in a home-construction firm)

Sequential interdependencies—where work must flow from one unit to another in a clearly defined sequence (e.g., assembly line)

Reciprocal interdependencies—where units must adjust to each other (e.g., sales and design groups tailor a product or service to customer needs)

Information technologies (Morton, 1991), as well as production and service technologies, can produce variations in interdependencies. Computer networking and electronic mail technologies, for example, encourage and facilitate reciprocal interdependencies among users, whereas older techniques for processing data on mainframe computers encouraged pooled or sequential relations among users. Work and information interdependencies may cross organizational boundaries and occur within them. Consider the interdependencies between the external suppliers of computer services to a governmental agency and the agency's computer staff. The external computer people may work independently of the internal staff—for example, when repairing a faulty mainframe drive. On other jobs, such as the installation of a networking system, the two staffs will be interdependent.

When the technology creates pooled interdependencies, operations can be coordinated by rules, standard operating procedures (e.g., "Discard parts that exceed standard by .003mm"), and supervision from above. When work must flow sequentially, rules and procedures must be supplemented by more detailed planning of the relations among units, closer monitoring of unit outputs, and more supervision from above. But these familiar coordination mechanisms do not fit the requirements of technologies that create reciprocal interdependencies between units. Coordination mechanisms that build in lateral relations between units best fit these needs for two-way communication and mutual adjustment. These mechanisms include teams, committees, and flexible, integrative roles, such as product managers and coordinators of interorganizational projects.

To examine fits between technological interdependencies and coordination mechanisms, practitioners can observe operations and conduct interviews about workflows between units that must work together. Interunit coordination is problematic if members view these coordination procedures as clumsy or inadequate, or if interunit contacts are characterized by frequent interruptions, misunderstandings, surprises, and high levels of conflict. In such cases members may not be adequately using current coordinating mechanisms, or these mechanisms may be inappropriate to the interdependencies between units.

Organic Versus Mechanistic Systems

This well-known typology provides the basis of a model for assessing the fits between the administrative system (structure, processes, and culture) of a division or organization and its environment, technology, and personnel (Burns & Stalker, 1961; Gresov, 1989; Lawrence & Lorsch, 1969; Tichy, 1983; Tushman & Nadler, 1978). The model can also be applied to smaller organizational units.

The main features of the typology and the conditions under which good fit occurs appear in Table 4.2 (derived partly from Tichy, 1983, p. 276). Organic systems provide greater information-processing capacity, encourage creativity and innovativeness, and facilitate rapid, flexible responses to change. Organic systems also provide more interesting and challenging work environments than mechanistic systems. On the other hand, they are costlier and harder to administer. Hence mechanistic systems usually are more efficient and productive than organic ones in units that perform high-volume, low-variance tasks. Units performing tasks of this sort usually face fairly predictable external conditions and do not have to carry on extensive contacts with external units.

Organizations that start out as entrepreneurial ventures usually have more organic administrative systems. They may retain these systems as they move into the Collectivity Stage in the organizational life cycle, in which group solidarity becomes important, but creativity and innovation continue to be emphasized (Bartunek & Louis, 1988; Quinn & Cameron, 1983). Administrators introduce more mechanistic systems as their organizations move into a third life-cycle stage that stresses formalization, control, and efficiency of operations. If formalization becomes unworkable, organizations may enter a Structural Elaboration stage in which they can differentiate between organic and mechanistic subunits.

To use the model in diagnosis, practitioners need to assess how organic or mechanistic a division's current administrative system is and how well the current system fits the conditions and effectiveness criteria listed in Table 4.1. Practitioners can measure employee expectations directly (chapter 3) or approximate them in terms of the level of education and training of the workforce. Interviews or questionnaires such as the Organizational Assessment Inventory (Van de Ven & Ferry, 1980; Appendix B) can assess the routineness of the technology, environmental predictability, and extent of external dependencies. Other techniques for assessing environmental conditions are discussed in chapter 5.

Standardized measures can facilitate the assessment of many of the administrative features summarized in Table 4.2. Separate indices can be created for each of the descriptive dimensions shown in the upper half of the table or a single combined index can be constructed. One advantage of examining each dimension separately is that low levels of

Table 4.2
Conditions Affecting the Fit of Mechanistic and Organic Systems

System Feature	*Mechanistic*	*Organic*
Roles, Responsibilities	Specialized, clearly defined.	Diffuse, flexible, change through use.
Coordination and Control	Supervision, rules, standard procedures; detailed plans, frequent evaluation based on clear objectives, standards.	Consultation among all having related tasks; flexible plans, diffuse, changing goals, evaluation over longer periods.
Communication	Top-down emphasis; top management has key outside contacts.	Multidirectional, multilevel contacts with outside.
Supervision and Leadership	Nonparticipative, one-on-one, loyalty to superiors stressed; position and experience grant authority.	Participative, stress on task, team, organization; expertise and knowledge grant authority.
Sources of Knowledge	Local, internal.	External, professional, cosmopolitan.
Fit best when		
Work processes are . . .	Routine (well understood, standardized).	Nonroutine (not well understood or designed for each problem.)
Task environment is . . .	Simple, predictable.	Complex, unpredictable.
External coordination is . . .	Limited.	Extensive.
Personnel expect . . .	High structuring and routine, control from above.	Role flexibility, challenging work, autonomy.
Life-cycle stage is . . .	Formalization and control.	Entrepreneurial or collectivity.
Effectiveness criteria stress . . .	Efficiency; standard, reliable operations; control from top or outside.	Creativity, innovation, adaptation, quality of work life, human resource development.

fit may be found between these administrative dimensions. For example, a division head might try to encourage managers to work together on innovative projects but inadvertently block teamwork by retaining a one-on-one style of supervision.

Taken as a whole, systems organized along traditional, bureaucratic principles may be judged too mechanistic if they face very unpredictable environments—for example, where customer preferences change suddenly in response to fads and fashions—and nonroutine tasks—for example, in new product development or scientific research. In particular, a division may need a more organic system if it is unable to cope with the following four types of challenges:

1. Adapt to change and respond rapidly and decisively to threats and opportunities.
2. Handle nonroutine tasks in innovative and creative ways.
3. Meet employee expectations for creative, challenging work.
4. Coordinate relations with other units and organizations.

Unless staff development, intrinsic motivation, and employee satisfaction are critical, divisions that use organic arrangements to deal with predictable environments, limited external dependencies, and routine tasks probably fail to take advantage of efficiencies that could be obtained by introducing more mechanistic procedures. If a preliminary application of the model suggests that change is needed in either direction, practitioners can focus more closely on the design tools that clients can most easily use as levers for change.

Divisionalization

A key question in the diagnosis of the structure of total organizations and divisions concerns the ways that units are grouped. When consultants examine an organization's current form of divisionalization, they should investigate whether people and units that must work closely together are grouped in the same administrative units or in close contact to one another. In addition, they should consider whether the structure keeps costs to a minimum by avoiding unnecessary duplication of positions and underuse of resources and provides sufficient adaptiveness to variations in markets and other environmental conditions (e.g., degree of governmental regulation of products or production processes). As a rule, organizations whose divisions form along functional lines (e.g., marketing, engineering, production) are less able to respond to divergences in markets and other environmental conditions than those whose divisions are made in terms of products and services (e.g., life, home, and commercial insurance divisions), or in terms of markets or geographical areas (Mintzberg, 1979). However, there are many variations within types and many opportunities for combining them.

Differentiation and Integration

The more the tasks, technology, and environments of divisions or other major subunits vary from one another, the more the divisional structures must be differentiated (Lawrence & Lorsch, 1969). For example, in a clothing firm with a division catering to the fashion trade (unpredictable environment) and one supplying uniforms to hospitals and other institutions (stable environment), the fashion division needs to be more organic than the division supplying uniforms. The need for differentiation also stems from many other types of divergences in tasks, environments, and workforce, such as legal conditions, levels of training of the workforce, and the size of production runs. To assess whether an organization is sufficiently differentiated, practitioners need to decide whether each division is allowed to adapt sufficiently to its own objectives, technology, environment, and personnel. Too much differentiation occurs if there are unjustifiable divergences in the administrative practices of various divisions.

Once organizations become differentiated internally, they face serious problems of integration (coordination) across divisions (Lawrence & Lorsch, 1969). If an organization is highly differentiated, the mechanistic forms of coordination and control listed in Table 4.2 are not likely to provide sufficient levels of integration. To accommodate great divergence among divisions, top management can grant them greater autonomy and monitor divisional financial results or create more lateral linkages between units and divisions that must work together (Mintzberg, 1979; Galbraith, 1977; Tichy, 1983). The following list arranges popular forms of lateral integration from the least to the most complex:

1. Direct contact between units.
2. Integrator and liaison roles (e.g., coordinator of hospital geriatric services).
3. Task forces and committees that temporarily unite members of several units.
4. Project groups and teams that make these links more permanent.
5. Matrix structures with dual (functional and project) authority lines.

Complex lateral integrating mechanisms can help organizations coordinate highly differentiated operations and cope with nonroutine technologies and unpredictable environments. On the other hand, they are costly and hard to administer (Bartlett & Ghoshal, 1990; Davis & Lawrence, 1977; Galbraith, Lawler, et al., 1993). Consultants and managers should, therefore, weigh carefully the possibilities for using simpler lateral coordination mechanisms or increasing divisional autonomy before considering elaborate, risky reorganizations along project and matrix lines.

Linkages With Other Organizations

When managers seek to reduce operating costs and increase their firm's flexibility within its markets, they may prefer to engage in contractual ties with external suppliers of services rather than producing goods and services within their own organization. Long-standing ties with outside organizations can also take the form of *network ties*—such as the ongoing relations between authors and publishers or cooperation among small contractors in the building trades (Powell, 1990). External ties can also be formalized in *strategic alliances* such as joint ventures, industry consortia, licensing arrangements, or acquisitions (Buono, 1991). In the extreme, the partners in an alliance can merge to form a single new firm. More and more organizations are developing strategic alliances as their managers seek to move quickly into international markets and take advantage of the capital, knowledge, or local access offered by alliance partners.

External linkages pose two sets of issues for diagnosis. First, consultants may be asked to help managers decide whether the anticipated benefits of the creation or retention of external linkages outweigh their disadvantages and potential risks. Although many of the business issues of relevance lay beyond the province of the behavioral sciences, diagnostic practitioners can facilitate decision making about strategic alliances and other external linkages. Practitioners can conduct diagnostic workshops in which decision makers are asked to review systematically the benefits they seek to achieve by proposed or current alliances and the risks and costs of such alliances. Practitioners may also survey or interview members of the many groups of stakeholders that are or will be affected by an alliance (Buono & Bowditch, 1990). This multiple-constituency approach provides top management with a more complex view of the issues to be weighed.

Interviews and surveys of the people involved in a merger or strategic alliance can explore the alliance's anticipated or current impact on administrative practices, the image and culture of the organizations, and the organizations' members (Buono & Bowditch, 1989). Alliances may affect the members of the organizations in many ways that can ultimately influence the success of the alliance and the overall performance of the partners to the alliance. People involved in a merger or other form of alliance may fear losing their job or organizational standing and may therefore refocus their efforts on their careers or on finding another job. They may also become embroiled in open and covert bargaining about their roles in the organization. Tension and conflicts may also develop between the staffs of the alliance partners. Feedback from such interviews or surveys can help top management plan steps that will facilitate the alliance and deal with the plurality of needs, cultural orientations, and interests among the employees who will take part in the new venture.

Second, both before and after the implementation of mergers and strategic alliances, diagnosis can assess the fit between the partners' administrative systems (structure, behavior, and processes), cultures, and human resources. The importance of achieving fits of these kinds increases with the need for administrative integration created by the alliance (Osborn & Baughn, 1993). *Specialist arrangements*—such as the exchange of a specific form of technology or a licensing agreement—do not typically require the parties to change their administrative practices very much. Nor need they shift their current structures, norms, and values. In contrast, *hybrid arrangements*—such as partial ownership arrangements or joint ventures aimed at developing a new set of products or new technologies—require higher levels of integration between the partners. Mergers require full integration between the partners. Practitioners must therefore determine how much integration is required between the strategic partners. For specialist arrangements, the diagnostic issue is whether current or planned coordination measures can ensure adequate cooperation. Hybrid arrangements and mergers pose two additional diagnostic issues: First, how good is the fit between the structures and cultures of the partners? Second, if fit is poor, do the managers within one of the organizations have the ability and desire to change their organization to achieve fit? If not, the alliance is likely to fail.

ACTUAL PRACTICES VERSUS OFFICIAL MANDATES

As in other forms of diagnosis, to examine many of the system fits listed in Table 4.1 practitioners need to distinguish between actual, ongoing patterns of behavior and official descriptions of organizational life.[3] Official descriptions can provide useful insights into management's image of the organization's desired state, but they cannot serve as data on organizational behavior in practice.

Examining Actual Practices

Actual practices can diverge greatly from official descriptions of these practices and from official purposes and procedures. Managers, for example, may report that they frequently consult with their subordinates before reaching important decisions, but the subordinates' own reports and other data sources on decision making may not confirm this idealized picture. What happens, for instance, when subordinates have bad news for their supervisors or hold different opinions (Argyris & Schon, 1978)? Other key processes—including controlling and rewarding (Lawler & Rhode, 1976), supervision, and conflict management (Pondy, 1967; Walton & Dutton, 1969)—should also be examined carefully.

Here is a listing of actual practices that practitioners may find diverge substantially from officially mandated ones:

1. Operative goals and priorities as shown by decisions about resource allocation (e.g., budgeting, staffing).
2. Unofficial structures (e.g., cliques, working ties that cut across departmental lines, end runs around immediate superiors to higher authorities; grapevines that bypass official communication channels).
3. Role definitions and group functions in practice (e.g., actual division of labor, definitions of tasks, responsibilities).
4. Informal leaders, influence patterns, and power relations.
5. Actual work procedures (e.g., uses of new technologies; recordkeeping and reporting practices; cutting corners on safety, quality checks; improvised solutions and procedures).
6. Everyday beliefs (culture) about the payoffs (or penalties) for hard work and initiative; perceptions of the tasks and conditions facing the organization (e.g., "We're about to get bought out. Quit while you can!"); beliefs about the kinds of information that can be taken seriously (e.g., "The forecasts from sales are always too optimistic.").

---

3. The terms *actual* behavior and behavior *in practice* are preferable to the more popular term *informal* behavior. The term *formalization* is often used to refer to the degree to which behavior and procedures are specified in writing (Daft, 1992, p. 13). Directives, goals, and structures can be official and authoritative without being formalized.

Collecting Data on Actual Practices

Since actual practices may run counter to official mandates, it is usually necessary to gather data on them through direct observations, intensive interviewing, or the analysis of organizational records. If respondents are especially cooperative and candid, data on ongoing social and working relations can be obtained using *sociometric questionnaires,* in which respondents name people or positions with whom they work closely or have frequent contact (Moch, Feather, & Fitzgibbons, 1983; Tichy, Tushman, & Fombrun, 1980). The patterns of one-way and mutual choice between respondents can be analyzed to provide maps of relations or simple statistical analyses of *network ties* (Nelson, 1988). Alternatively, investigators can incorporate questions about group leadership and work relations into open interviews.

Open or semistructured interviews should seek explicit descriptions of how respondents act in a range of work situations, rather than generalizations or expressions of attitudes, because explicit behavioral reports are somewhat less subject to bias than generalizations of expressions of attitudes. For instance, to obtain data about the actual division of labor within a project group, practitioners could ask several members to describe what each member of the group did during the design of a project and then draw the appropriate conclusion after examining all the data. This procedure is more likely to yield valid results than asking members to generalize about whether "responsibilities are clear" in the group or asking whether task assignments are flexible enough to allow for unforeseen circumstances.

Another fruitful strategy for examining actual practices is to gather data from interviews and organizational records about the whole path along which a service, product, client, or idea moves through the client organization. In a study of hospital coordination mechanisms, for example, investigators might trace the entire course of treatment of representative hospital patients, from reception to release. In a study of decision making and working relations in an industrial firm they could follow a new product from its earliest design stages to routine production.

The advantage of direct observations and the analysis of existing data is that much information may be obtained unobtrusively (Webb, Campbell, Schwartz, et al., 1966), without interfering with people's behavior or influencing it. For example, by observing attendance at meetings or by checking records, practitioners may discover that a project that has officially been assigned high priority is being neglected by senior staff members. Although such observational data can be very informative, their reliability may be low, and they are usually hard to quantify.

ASSESSING THE IMPACTS OF FITS

As Figure 4.1 suggests, consultants should assess the impacts of system fits directly rather than assuming, as some authors do (e.g., Beer, 1980; Nadler & Tushman, 1980a), that high levels of fit or system integration are always preferable. Instead, any particular pattern and level of fit can be assumed to have both costs and benefits that can be identified and weighed only in terms of specific effectiveness criteria. Take the assessment of gaps between official rules and actual behavior: The hoarding of supplies by units on a military base probably causes wastage and raises costs but may also contribute to solidarity and morale within units. In some instances outright violations of official procedures help employees do better work. For instance, Blau (1955, pp. 91-116) reports how employees in a federal agency improved the quality of their work and contributed to group solidarity when they broke rules forbidding them from consulting with their peers and requiring them to turn to their supervisors when problems arose. The discussion of empowerment below treats additional instances in which people can improve their performance by making use of unofficial relations and processes.

A further problem in assessing the effects of fit derives from the ability of many organizations to operate with fairly high levels of structural incongruity and inconsistency. Both for-profit and not-for-profit organizations can persist in a state of "permanent failure" in which they continue to enjoy budgetary or owner support, despite their low levels of performance and their failure to satisfy the expectations of clients or customers (Meyer & Zucker, 1989). In particular, there may be limited fit between actual practices and the official goals and programs of public service organizations. Such organizations often enjoy external legitimacy and financial support, even though they lack effective mechanisms for scanning external developments and responding to them. These types of *loose coupling* (Orton & Weick, 1990) thwart efforts to introduce efficiency, accountability, and responsiveness to public expectations. But these same arrangements also reduce interference by external pressure groups and regulators and thereby allow employees to carry out their work according to their professional standards (Meyer & Rowan, 1977).

System incongruities and lacks of fit can even contribute to organizational growth, innovation, and change. Some high-technology firms, for example, tolerate and even encourage overlaps between units, ambiguous definitions of unit goals and assignments, and high levels of in-fighting and politicking to sustain and encourage creativity and initiative (e.g., Kidder, 1981; Kunda, 1992). Lack of fit between parts of an organization or certain system elements may also occur because one functional unit or subgroup is more attuned to certain external or technological forces than another unit or group. In professional organizations such as hospitals and universities, for example, top administrators are often more aware of external financial constraints than are most of the professional staff. In contrast, the professionals are likely to be more sensitive to pressures to keep up with scientific and technological developments than their administrators. Such tensions between individuals and subgroups may reflect and foster creativity, innovation, and adaptation to external change (Burns, 1961; Robbins, 1978). If clients and practitioners value these organizational states, they would be unwise to try to force system elements into tight alignment. Judged in terms of their impact on innovativeness and adaptation to change, the fits in many organizations turn out to be too tight, rather than too loose (Katz & Kahn, 1978, p. 174).

Finally, in assessing fit, practitioners should keep in mind that many tasks and organizational needs can be handled in more than one way. Hence there is room for variation within the recurring organizational types—such as the organic and mechanistic systems—observed by consultants and researchers (Van de Ven & Drazin, 1985). For all of these reasons, consultants should assess system fits and lacks of fit in terms of explicit effectiveness criteria. They can decide whether a lack of fit between certain system elements or parts of an organization is detrimental and what steps, if any, should be taken to improve fits.

POWER RELATIONS AND PROCESSES

Power relations and influence processes are among the most important types of actual behavior to examine in diagnosis. Even if an understanding of political processes and power distribution does not lead directly to proposals for organizational improvement, it can greatly help consultants manage the consulting process (Greiner & Schein, 1988; Harrison, 1991). The following typical war story (Quinn, 1977, p. 23) illustrates the potential impact of power on efforts to introduce organizational change.

Case 9

A major textile fibers company had constant fights between strong managers in the divisions of marketing, production, and research and development. Yet when the creation of product-management teams was proposed to "coordinate the very things that caused the friction," the feuding managers formed a powerful coalition to resist the innovation.

The terms *power* and *influence* refer interchangeably here to the capacity to get things done, including the ability to get people to do things that they might otherwise not do (Finkelstein, 1992; Kanter, 1977; Mintzberg, 1983, p. 5). Political actions—attempts to achieve desired outcomes—often aim to influence budgeting decisions and other forms of resource allocation, to shape goals and programs, to promote or resisting personnel changes, and to determine the resolution of conflicts and crises (Burns, 1961; Pfeffer, 1981b; Zald & Berger, 1978).

As suggested in chapter 2, when consultants understand an organization's power structure and politics, they may be able to work in ways that fit these political realities without compromising the consulting process. If consultants ignore these realities, they are likely to encounter resistance to their diagnoses and may recommend interventions with negative consequences or that cannot be implemented. In Case 9, for example, the proposed product-management teams would have drawn members from each of the three functional divisions. But this scheme could only work if the division managers were willing to surrender some autonomy. Innovations such as quality circles for production or clerical workers also cannot be implemented successfully unless supervisors and managers are willing to give real power to the members of quality circles. Furthermore, where substantial power differences and fundamental conflicts of interest prevail, many popular organization-development techniques—including process consultation, and team building—cannot be used because they require high levels of trust and interpersonal openness (Harrison, 1991; Huff, 1980; G. Strauss, 1976; Tushman, 1977).

Diagnosing the Distribution and Uses of Power

Outcomes of Influence Processes

One problem facing consultants is the assessment of the consequences of people's efforts to use power to influence others and to attain particular ends. Rather than assuming that any attempt to shape or manipulate others is by definition undesirable, consultants need to acknowledge the essentially political nature of organizational life and look directly at the effects of influence processes. Organizations' members may use their power to oppose change, as in Case 9, or to press for change (Burns, 1961). In many organizations proposals for new products and other innovations are accepted only when powerful managers work hard to convince decision makers to provide the resources needed to develop a new idea and fight to overcome opposition to its implementation (Kanter, 1983). In some instances such champions of new concepts have violated official directives and procedures by diverting resources to new product development (Peters and Waterman, 1982).

Practitioners can only evaluate political activity from the viewpoints of particular actors within the organization and in terms of clear effectiveness criteria. Consider, for example, a situation in which workers marshal the support of local politicians to delay the closing of an unprofitable plant long enough for the drafting of reorganization proposals by joint labor-management committees. A management consultant who concentrated on improving the firm's profitability would regard the workers' actions a threat to the firm's effectiveness. In contrast, a consultant to the workers would probably view their actions favorably (e.g., Alinsky, 1971; Chesler, Crawfoot, & Bryant, 1978), as might a consultant to management who placed greater stress on job security and the standing of the firm in the community.

Influence Tactics

It is important to assess the effects of the tactics people use to influence others as well as to evaluate the outcomes of these efforts. People who have formal authority or control over valued resources may try to influence others and accomplish things by changing the flow of material and social rewards and sanctions to others. Other influence tactics include appealing to logic and common standards and manipulating people by providing them with selective information about a situation or creating indirect pressures to act in a particular fashion (Benfari & Knox, 1991; Porter, Allen, & Angle, 1981). To assess the effects of such influence tactics and other uses of power, practitioners need to consider issues such as:

- How do those subject to a particular influencing tactic react to it?
- Does the use of this tactic increase tensions or conflicts between groups?
- Do reliance on personal loyalties and political deal making undercut the organization's stress on performance or professional excellence?

- Do the methods used to resolve conflicts produce lasting solutions that are regarded as fair?

Empowerment

People and groups use power to accomplish tasks and fulfill organizational objectives as well as to oppose them. Hence a critical issue for diagnosis concerns the degree to which particular groups are empowered—in the sense of having sufficient resources and influence to accomplish their tasks. Women and members of minority groups often lack the power to get things done within organizations. This disadvantage can stem from the common practice of shunting women and minorities into dead-end clerical, service, and production jobs. These jobs provide limited power and opportunities for advancement (Kanter, 1977; Mills & Tancred, 1992). Women and minorities can also suffer from an inability to gain access to informal channels of influence, such as personal and familial contacts with powerful administrators.

Entire units or strata within an organization, not just subgroups, can also suffer from lack of power. First-line supervisors, for example, often cannot do their jobs adequately because they cannot control or influence the lines of supply to their units, lack vital organizational information, and cannot advance within the organization (Kanter, 1979). Because of their lack of power, these supervisors become resistant to managerial initiatives, administer programs mechanistically, and achieve low productivity. Middle managers also need to acquire power to do their jobs well (e.g., Izraeli, 1975), and staff specialists, such as behavioral scientists and planners, often lack both the formal authority and the informal standing needed to get their ideas implemented (e.g., Phillips, 1991). To promote innovation, management must empower people who are capable of developing new ideas and technologies (Delbecq & Mills, 1985; Kanter, 1983). Consultants need, therefore, to be on the lookout for situations like these where group and divisional effectiveness can be enhanced by giving people more control of needed resources and easier access to important information and to key decision makers.

Power Distribution

One way to decide whether units have enough power is to examine the overall power distribution in a division or organization. When power is highly centralized, control over important resources and decisions is concentrated in the higher ranks of the organization. Here is a list of possible consequences of shifting toward a more decentralized distribution of authority and power (Child, 1977; Carlisle, 1974; Khandwalla, 1977; Kanter, 1983; Mills, 1991; but note the complexities cited by Huber, Miller, & Glick, 1991):

POSITIVE CONSEQUENCES OF DECENTRALIZATION

- Reduced burden on top management to make decisions and process information
- Cost savings from reduction in administrative levels and paperwork
- Improved information flow and decision quality
- Enhanced ability of middle managers to solve problems on their own
- Flexible and rapid response to local conditions (e.g., in multinational firm)
- Improved morale
- More innovation
- More responsibility for results among lower ranks
- Better management development

NEGATIVE CONSEQUENCES

- Reduction in top management's ability to forge a unifying strategy and to respond quickly to change
- Increased costs for training, compensation, capital equipment, and plant
- Duplication of positions
- Creation of local power centers
- Heightened conflict between units

To diagnose the distribution of power, practitioners should assess the degree to which the organization (or unit) is decentralized and weigh the probable costs and benefits of changing the power distribution in light of explicit effectiveness criteria. Practitioners and clients are more likely to favor decentralization when an organization's subunits must be able to respond rapidly and appropriately to local and specialized problems. These capacities are particularly critical when organizations are very large and geographically dispersed; environments are very complex, competitive, and changing rapidly; and many tasks cannot be routinized.

Investigating Power Relations and Processes

Indicators of Power and Influence[4]

Gathering trustworthy information on power relations and processes is a challenge to organizational consultants. First, they need to decide which people and groups have acted or might act in ways that could

4. This section draws substantially on Pfeffer's (1981b, pp. 35-65) discussion of assessing power. See also Finkelstein (1992).

influence the consulting process or the organizational features being studied. In addition to high-ranking managers, interest groups (stakeholders) may converge along the lines of departments, occupations, ranks, and social characteristics (e.g., sex, ethnic background). Naturally, actors concerned with one issue, such as the redesign of jobs, may be different from those concerned with another, such as budget allocations. Once investigators have identified the key issues and actors, they can chart their relations, showing the key actors for each issue, their position on the issue, coalitions and other links among these actors, and their relative power (Savage, Nix, Whitehead, & Blair, 1991).

Practitioners can try to learn how much power various actors have and how they use that power. To assess power and its uses directly necessitates following the treatment of specific issues in different parts of the organization and examining political struggles directly. Since this kind of information is rarely available, it is usually necessary to look for overt manifestations of power (Kanter, 1977). Table 4.3 takes this approach in providing questions about the power relations and suggesting techniques for gathering relevant information. The questions in the table usually refer to individuals and formal and informal groups, but they may also refer to the power of social and cultural subgroups or to gender patterns. If some actors appear to be powerful according to one set of criteria listed in the table (e.g., status symbols), but not according to another (e.g., access to top decision makers), investigators will need to obtain additional information to determine whether some of the indicators of power are invalid or whether there are several distinct power bases but no single group of powerful actors.

Data-Collection Techniques

The sensitivity and subtlety of political processes makes them hard to measure with questionnaires. Still, some authors have developed questionnaires for identifying powerful groups or individuals, delineating coalitions, describing prevalent influence tactics, and measuring power distribution (Enz, 1989; Moch, Cammann, & Cooke, 1983; Nelson, 1988; Price & Mueller, 1986; Tannenbaum, 1968; chapter 3 on MOAQ and OAI). As Table 4.3 suggests, a wide range of qualitative and largely unobtrusive techniques can be used as alternatives or supplements to questionnaires.

Some of the strategies and methods listed in Table 4.3 can also provide data on the uses of power and its distribution. If practitioners can observe the meetings of major decision-making forums, for example,

Table 4.3
Who Is Powerful?

Focal Area and Guiding Questions	*Research Strategies and Methods*
Resources: What kinds of resources are most important to members—funds, equipment personnel, information, knowledge? Which groups get disproportionate shares?	Observe (and/or interview on) key resources and distribution, status symbols; examine budget allocations.
Who controls distribution?	Examine organization charts, job descriptions; interview.
Centrality: What technical and administrative processes are vital to everyday operations? What processes are critical to organizational success? Who influences and participates in them?	Interview unit heads; study organization charts, job descriptions; analyze reports from interviews and workshops on crises, failures, successes.
Who handles contacts with powerful external organizations, units, and groups?	Interview; examine organization charts; survey (i.e., give questionnaires) to members, heads of units about contacts.
Who is regarded as irreplaceable?	Interview knowledgeable members; survey members of relevant units.
Structure: Who holds the top positions (titles) in the hierarchy? How many titles does each person have? How much is the person paid compared to others in the organization? What share of ownership does she/he have?	Examine organization charts, reports, and records; interview.
Participation and Influence in Decision Making: Who participates in key (official and unofficial) decision-making forums? Who has access to top decision makers?	Examine organization charts, job descriptions, reports on membership in forums; observe participation; interview on access, participation.
Whose views dominated major decisions? Who won in power struggles and conflicts?	Analyze decisions reported in documents, press, interviews, workshops.
To whom do members turn for sponsorship of new ideas, projects?	Interview; analyze successes, failures reported in interviews, workshops.
Reputation: Which units and individuals are regarded as especially powerful?	Survey members for ranking of units and influential people; interview; observe attention, deference granted to individuals.
Which units do members join so as to get ahead fast? With whom do members try to develop relationships? Whom do they try to impress?	Interview; examine executives' career lines to find units that provide avenues to the top.

they may obtain invaluable data on how members resolve differences and conflicts and the degree to which top executives share power with subordinates. Unfortunately, many influence processes occur outside of such formal gatherings and are hard to observe.

To gather data on influence processes, consultants often have to rely on interviews or discussions during meetings or workshops. In workshops or interviews consultants may ask members to provide detailed accounts of organizational successes, the resolution of past organizational problems and crises, and accounts of the treatment of new ideas or proposals. In providing these accounts, members may, of course, justify and improve upon their own behavior and that of others to whom they are loyal. They may exaggerate the failings of those they hold in low esteem. Still, when conducted and analyzed with sensitivity to these possibilities, interviews and group discussions can provide insight into members' perceptions of political processes, key political actors, and the kinds of influence tactics used within the organization. To develop an understanding of power relations and processes that is independent of the perceptions of particular organizational members, practitioners will have to carefully cross-check members' reports with one another and with other kinds of information.

EXERCISES

1. Assessing Fits

In this exercise you may draw on your prior knowledge of an organization or gather Basic Organizational Information and conduct several General Orientation Interviews before beginning the exercise. On a large sheet of newsprint make a matrix listing as rows and columns all eight of the system elements. Subdivide the Inputs (Resources) category into three categories—People (human resources), Knowledge and Information, and Material Resources. The matrix should be 10 by 10 with 45 cells above the diagonal. For each cell, ask how well the row entry (e.g., human resources) fits with the column entry (e.g., knowledge and informational resources). To make these queries more concrete, look at the questions about fit in Table 4.1. Where no question appears in the table, suggest your own. For example, do employees (human resources) have the knowledge needed to perform their tasks? If not, can they readily obtain it? Make notes on the degree of fit between each pair in your matrix. Be explicit about your criteria to assess fit. Once you have completed the matrix, note the two cases of poor fit that seem to be most harmful to effectiveness. Be clear about your effectiveness criteria. Write a report on these two cases in which you explain the nature of the lack of fit and its impacts and make suggestions for improving the fits.

2. Actual Practices: Rewards

Interview the head and at least one subordinate in a department or division. Use a list of guiding, open-ended questions about rewards and their relation to other features of the unit. In addition to writing your own questions, you may want to use the following items listed in Appendix A: I-1 and 2; II-1; III-1, 2, and 3; IV-2; VI-1, 2, 5, and 6; VII-1, 2, 3, 6, 7, 8, and 9; VIII-1, 2, and 3; IX-1 and 3; XI-1, 2, and 3. Cover the following issues in your interviews and discuss each of them in your report:

1. What are the main official types of rewards and sanctions and what other rewards and sanctions are used in practice?
2. What kinds of behavior are subject to rewards and sanctions? (Be specific.)
3. What types of actions are encouraged and discouraged? Consider hard work versus taking it easy, personal loyalty to supervisors and peers, risk taking, exercising initiative, generating new ideas, cooperation with others within or outside the unit.
4. Are the same rewards offered to everyone or can people receive different types of rewards that are more appealing to them? (e.g., One person may want a bonus, while another wants a chance to earn a degree while working.)
5. How do each of the following influence the current system of rewards—peers, supervisor, higher level management, labor agreements?
6. If you have sufficient information, assess the fits between the current reward system and other system elements (see Table 4.1).

3. Power to Act

Use at least two of the approaches listed in Table 4.3 to determine which people have the most power within some subunit of an organization such as a branch, a division, or a department. Interview two of them about a major problem or challenge facing their unit. Find out during the interview or by another method whether they have the resources needed to deal with the problem. If not, specify what resources they would need to take action and what could be done to help them attain these resources or solve the problem some other way.

5

Diagnosing Environmental Relations

The first part of the chapter shows how to examine the environmental conditions facing an organization and the management of external relations. Techniques for conducting intensive interviews are discussed along with other data-gathering methods. A discussion follows of Open Systems Planning, a technique that gives clients most of the responsibility for diagnosing their organization's position in its environment and for planning actions to improve this position.

International joint ventures, European unification, fiber-optic technologies, national computer networking, health reforms, new energy taxes, the emergence of single-parent families, the aging of the populations of Europe and the United States—the mass media provide a lengthy and rapidly changing list of developments that challenge today's organizations. Practitioners of diagnosis can make a major contribution to organizational effectiveness by helping decision makers identify the external conditions that affect their organization, assess current tactics for managing environmental relations, and find ways to take advantage of external changes and improve their organization's competitive position.

This chapter shows practitioners how to conduct such a diagnosis of environmental relations. Managers may also use this type of diagnosis to improve decision making and planning without the aid of consultants. The diagnostic models and techniques discussed here apply best to entire organizations or semiautonomous divisions but can also be adapted to less autonomous units. The lower the autonomy of a focal unit, the more its environment includes other units within the larger organization—including units at the same level in the hierarchy and top management.

GUIDELINES FOR DIAGNOSIS

Here are guidelines for conducting a thorough diagnosis of environmental relations:

1. *Identify the key conditions in the task environment of the client organization (or unit).* These conditions include markets, sectoral and industry-wide conditions, relevant technical and scientific conditions, labor pools, regulation, and the behavior of competitors. Key conditions for a firm providing telecommunications services, for example, include the market for its products, the state of competition within the field, the state of telecommunications technology, governmental regulations, availability and cost of access to satellites and other communications facilities, and the pool of available talent from which the firm recruits. The external constituencies that have a stake in an organization's affairs and try to influence its operations may include environmental and political groups that favor or oppose the use of particular sites for transmission facilities as well as national public-interest groups concerned with issues such as minority employment, employee health, and women's rights. Public agencies and service organizations are especially subject to pressures and constraints from external regulatory and certifying bodies (Fottler, 1981; Meyer & Rowan, 1977).

2. *Assess the organization's strategic position in its environment in terms of its ability to obtain resources and dispose of outputs on favorable terms* (Andrews, 1971; Porter, 1980). Indicators of strategic position include rates of growth in resources and revenues, market share, and external ratings and reputation. *Strategic advantage* often derives from the ability to provide a product or service that is superior in price, quality, or terms of delivery than those offered by the competition—or in being their sole supplier. To obtain an advantage over potential competitors, organizations need to exploit their distinctive capacities to the fullest. For instance, partners in a law firm might avoid competing directly with prestigious firms that specialize in local business contracts. Instead they could obtain a strategic advantage by developing expertise in very specialized fields, such as international contracts, that were underrepresented in their area. The strategic position of many public organizations stems from their being the sole supplier of a particular service. But a growing range of public-sector organizations must compete with other not-for-profit organizations or with for-profit firms for clientele, personnel, funds, public approval, and legal authority to provide particular services.

3. *Describe the main organizations with which the client organization interacts and its relations with them.* Outside organizations may include suppliers, consumers of goods and services, supervisory and regulatory groups, unions, competitors, community and political groups that have a stake in the organization's actions, and nonmanaging owners (e.g.,

stockholders). Relations can range from competition to cooperation (see chapter 4 on linkages with other organizations). They can also include hierarchical links such as supervision and ownership. To examine the focal organization's power in relation to outside organizations, practitioners can assess its dependence on these external organizations for vital resources and the dependence of these organizations on the client organizations. *Resource dependence* gives the supplier of the needed resource power over the recipient (Pfeffer & Salancik, 1978).

4. *Note the main units and individuals who handle external contacts.* Besides noting formal responsibilities for functions such as sales, public relations, fundraising, and staff recruitment, practitioners can examine which people or groups fill these roles in practice. Techniques such as responsibility charting (chapter 4) may prove useful if there is confusion or disagreement about who handles critical external relations.

5. *Describe the demands and pressures stemming from the environment and the resulting opportunities and problems facing the organization.* Each external group or condition can be thought of as pressing the organization to act in a particular fashion. A city council may be pressing its Youth Services Division to cut back on staff, while community groups demand fuller services and greater involvement in decision making. Acquiescence to a demand for community involvement in decision making would probably require changes in administrative processes and disrupt routines. In contrast, external developments may offer opportunities, including expansion or diversification of services or sales, acquisition of new forms of knowledge or technology, improvement of political standing and influence over the environment, and enhanced recruitment of personnel.

Besides examining the specific content of external forces, consultants should also evaluate the degree of predictability of important environmental developments. As suggested in chapter 4, mechanistic administrative procedures can more readily handle predictable environmental developments than rapidly changing, unpredictable ones. Environmental predictability shows up in the ability of members of the organization to anticipate changes in the flows of services, materials, or resources delivered to the environment and received from it during the past year or two. The Christmas rush is predictable at the post office, but holiday sales of clothing are somewhat less predictable. Other indications of predictability include the frequency of interruptions, exceptions, and problems associated with obtaining resources (i.e., inputs) and delivering goods and services (i.e., outputs) (Van de Ven and Ferry, 1980, pp. 141-158).

6. *Assess the impacts of external forces on system dynamics (growth, contraction, periodic adjustments); internal states (e.g., conflict, cohesion), and impacts on resource and output flows.* In addition to assessing the organization's overall environmental position (#1 above), practitioners can examine how specific external conditions or pressures affect system dynamics. For example, a sudden rise in interest rates can produce a radical decline in real estate sales. The growth of the environmental movement sharpened public resistance to the construction of nuclear power plants and created new opportunities for firms specializing in low-pollution energy sources. Political upheavals may disrupt a firm's ability to deliver its products or services, whereas improvements in communications technologies can enhance that ability.

7. *Examine the organization's responses to external problems and demands and its efforts to discover and take advantage of opportunities.* Practitioners should consider both the concrete actions taken in response to external demands and the implications of these actions for organization-environment relations. For example, the Director of Youth Services (see #5 above) could respond to the demand for greater community participation in decision making by informing the citizens' group that their request was being considered. This response might reduce external pressure and delay or avoid the need for a decisive response.

Organizations can respond to external pressures by making *internal adjustments* or by *intervening in the environment* to reduce pressures or shape demands at their source (see Child, 1977; Galbraith, 1977; Miles, 1980; Pfeffer & Salancik, 1978). As noted in chapter 2, *incremental actions,* whether internal or external, build on previous responses and do not require major investments or system changes, whereas *strategic actions* entail major internal changes or major efforts to intervene in the environment. Common types of internal adjustments include:

- Evading or delaying response to external demands and pressures
- Acceding to demands that least threaten organizational routines
- Limiting the impact of pressure groups by assigning responsibility for dealing with them to functions or units (e.g., customer relations) that are isolated from the rest of the organization and have limited impact on it
- Adjusting work procedures or flows to take account of changes in the availability of resources or the demand for services
- Monitoring external developments to reduce surprises and disruptions and to facilitate planning

- Making design changes (chapter 4) to improve organization-environment fits

For example, the heads of a junior college have a variety of options for coping with changes in computer technology and a growing student demand for computer training. They can monitor these developments by appointing a committee to study the problem, add an introductory course on computers, or incorporate computer skills into existing courses. In contrast, organizations intervene in their environments by:

- Lobbying and maneuvering for political support
- Using economic power (e.g., boycotts, pricing below market to drive out competitors) to influence external groups
- Advertising to shape demand or attitudes
- Cooperating with other organizations to share resources, reduce competition, and shape other environmental conditions
- Creating short- or long-term linkages with outside organizations (chapter 4)

Practitioners can also explore the ways that the organization's responses to external forces stem from members' *interpretations* of their environment and their relations to it. Shared norms and beliefs may encourage members to look for opportunities and challenges in the environment or to ignore external developments (Kotter & Heskett, 1992). Moreover, shared beliefs and norms can shape the choice of response to the environment. Take the case of organizational responses to signs of a downturn in performance (Ford & Baucus, 1987). Decision makers may favor ignoring these signs and riding out the downturn, making incremental adjustments, or taking strategic action to change internal or external conditions. The choice among these options and the particular steps chosen will reflect the decision makers' judgments concerning the likely length of the downturn, its severity, its causes, and their organization's capability to ride it out or to take strategic action to reverse the trend.

8. *Assess the effectiveness of current responses to the environment.* Consultants and their clients should evaluate internal adjustments and environmental interventions in terms of agreed-upon effectiveness criteria. In the case of the junior college, for example, no extra funds were available for computer training, so its costs would have to be balanced by increased revenues. Therefore, in terms of budgetary considerations, adding a course in computers that could attract additional students as

well as serve current students was a more effective response than introducing computer training into existing courses. Course enrollment fees could generate additional revenues, whereas the purchase of computer equipment for use in existing courses would add expenses without generating revenues.

The Adaptation and Resource Position criteria listed in Table 2.1 can serve as standards for evaluating the impacts of organizational efforts to manage external relations. These criteria emphasize the quality and quantity of resources obtained and the ability of the organization to adapt to external change (see also chapter 4, "Diagnosing System Fits"). In addition, effectiveness can be defined in terms of the organization's ability to create favorable external conditions in which to operate.

Practitioners can also evaluate the effectiveness of tactics for managing environmental relations in terms of their impact on internal processes. For example, if an organization uses tactics that limit external interference in the workflow, then routines can more readily be established and less expensive and complex forms of coordination can be used. If external forces create chronic problems and crises, or disruptions periodically reach major proportions, then current responses may be judged to be inadequate. Other signs of ineffective tactics include severe internal tensions and conflicts that result from external pressures, or the use of stop-gap techniques that delay serious management of external threats until they reach crisis proportions.

9. *Identify external trends that are creating new problems and opportunities or are likely to affect the organization in the future.* Environmental developments like those cited at the beginning of this chapter can create new problems and opportunities and make current forms of environmental management outmoded. By monitoring developments in the general environment, consultants and managers can sometimes anticipate and plan for likely impacts on the organization's immediate task environment. The demand for college courses in computers, for example, reflects changes in the computer industry that have led to the widespread acceptance of computers in the workplace and at home. Similarly, the aging of a community's population eventually reduces demand for services such as elementary education and pediatric medicine and generates demand for services in adult education and medical specializations such as internal medicine and geriatrics. No one can predict external developments adequately. Nonetheless, managers who follow developing trends may more readily take advantage of emerging opportunities and prepare to cope with emerging threats.

10. *Look for ways to improve the management of current environmental relations and possible responses to anticipated developments.* Consultants and clients should first consider ways to enhance current tactics for managing external relations. For instance, a national park that suffers from overcrowding during peak season can spread use over a wider area by requiring campground reservations and restricting access to overcrowded sites. If effectiveness cannot be achieved by incremental actions, two types of long-run strategic changes can be considered. First, the client organization might reorganize by making basic changes in its structure, processes, technology, resource acquisitions and allocations, or even in its culture. Changes in organization design and far-reaching organizational transformations require substantial investments of time and money and often produce unanticipated and undesirable effects on system elements and subcomponents that were not direct targets for change. The introduction of new forms of automation in manufacturing, for example, may increase the importance of those functions charged with monitoring and controlling the automated operations and thereby lead to conflicts between this new interest group and older occupational groups. Hence, in considering the possibility of reorganization, consultants and managers need to pay attention to the organization's readiness and capacity for change and weigh the expected benefits of reorganizations against their potential costs and negative consequences (chapter 2). A useful way to assess likely consequences is to examine the ways in which reorganizations will affect fits between system elements.

Second, the organization can reduce external constraints and improve its environmental standing by redefining its goals and strategies so as to alter one or more of its environmental domains—by entering a new field of business or market, by changing its mix of products and service, or by changing the basis of competition (e.g., service versus price). A real estate firm specializing in home sales might begin to handle commercial or institutional properties. A municipal hospital might begin to offer laboratory or diagnostic services at private-sector rates to patients who would not otherwise be eligible for the hospital's services.

Practitioners and clients can evaluate such possibilities in terms of risks and their probable impacts on the organization's strategic position and its resource flows. If, for instance, the directors of a new art museum seek to attract donations and public support in a city that already has a well-established art museum, they may look for new areas of distinctive competence for the new museum. They could develop collections in areas where the veteran museum has few holdings or offer special educational services to the public. To choose between these alternatives, decision makers must carefully weigh the probable costs, risks, and likely outcomes of each course of action. Although some not-for-profit organizations can shift environmental domains in this fashion, others cannot do so because of their charter, public pressures, or their commitments to a particular organizational identity and mission.

DIAGNOSTIC METHODS

Data Gathering

Direct Investigation

If possible, practitioners should gather data from important clients and other members of the focal organization's environment in much the same ways that they obtain information from members of the focal organization. Direct investigations of the environment can help members of the client organization look at their strengths and weaknesses through the eyes of powerful groups in their environment (Morgan, 1988).

Consultants may interview key clients, customers, and even competitors and representatives of stakeholder groups. For example, a diagnostic practitioner might interview the head of an environmental defense group that opposes expansion of the client's physical plant. Outside experts can also be consulted on topics such as the state of the industry or sector in which the client organization operates.

As the following case suggests, interviews with members of the organization's environment can sometimes shed light on critical organization-environment relations and stimulate efforts to improve these relations:

Case 10

As part of an organizational diagnosis focused on quality improvement, the human resources specialist in a high-technology firm asked key customers to assess the firm's performance. Interviews with customers covered their involvement in the development of new products and assessed the support and service received after delivery. Feedback from these interviews to line managers within the firm helped them understand the importance of quality management and served as a stimulus for improvements in product development, support, and service.

Valuable information about external conditions and relations can also be obtained from the daily press and business publications, information sources such as *Standard & Poor's* (Kinnear & Taylor, 1987, pp. 152-163, 177-188), and organizational documents. Documentation may also be available on sectors such as health, social services, and education in which many public organizations and not-for-profit organizations operate. Practitioners can also consult outside experts on topics such as the state of an industry or technology. Additional data may come from market research and business planning studies conducted before the diagnostic study. Moreover, if marketing issues are especially critical to the diagnosis, consultants may suggest that clients further investigate business or marketing conditions before deciding to change their products or services or to move into a new environmental domain.

Indirect Investigation

Unfortunately, practical constraints and considerations of client discretion often prevent direct access to people outside of the client organization. In such cases, practitioners gather information about environmental relations primarily through interviews with top management and other officials with responsibility for handling specific types of external relations (e.g., sales, public relations, customer service, fundraising). These interviews can include questions like those in Appendix A, sections IV and V, which deal with organization-environment fits.

Constructing an Interview Guide

Rather than preparing set questions in advance, investigators with experience in semistructured interviewing may prefer to gather data on environmental relations as well as on other system features through interviews based on an interview guide (Schatzman & Strauss, 1973). The guide lists all the topics to be investigated and then allows the interviewer to frame each question to reflect the distinctive circumstances of the client organization and to take into account previous answers. Interview guides thus ensure coverage of major topics while allowing flexibility. But interview guides have lower reliability because they allow for more variation between interviews and between interviews. Using interview guides also requires more interviewer skill than does the use of more structured schedules.

A guide designed to cover key aspects of external relations as viewed by members of the client organization might contain the following major headings:

1. Key external conditions—markets, fields, competition.
2. Strategic position—access to resources, demand for outputs, competitive advantage.
3. Main outside organizations, types of relations (ties, competition versus cooperation, resource dependence).
4. Main units, people who handle external contacts.
5. Demands, pressures from outside; resulting opportunities, problems.
6. System impacts—growth, decline, adjustments, internal effects (e.g., conflict), impacts on resource flows, output flows (product/services).
7. Current management of problems, demands, opportunities; internal adjustments, environmental interventions; incremental versus strategic actions.
8. Effectiveness of current actions.
9. External trends affecting the organization; future problems, opportunities.
10. Steps to improve current management of environment, possible future actions.

Each major heading in the guide would be broken down into subheadings to cover particular issues. For example, items 7 and 8 could be specified as:

7. Current management of problems, demands, opportunities.
   - 7-1. Specific actions—describe in detail. What is/was done, by whom? (Look for internal adjustments, interventions in environment; incremental versus strategic actions.)
   - 7-2. Other actions (e.g., "Did your group make any other attempts to moderate these pressures/deflect these criticisms/anticipate such developments, etc.?" Interviewer, look for anticipatory versus reactive moves).
8. Effectiveness of current actions.
   - 8-1. Impact of actions on external actor, conditions (e.g., "How did x react to the steps you took?").

     Effectiveness (e.g.,"Did these steps improve your revenues?").
   - 8-2. Internal impacts. (Probe for felt effects of tactics, whether they produced desired results, how successful they seemed to respondent, and meaning of success for him/her.)
   - 8-3. Changes in tactics and impacts—Were similar problems handled in same way in the past? What happened after changes in tactics? (Probe for shifts in tactics, stance toward environment, variations in impacts.)

Naturally, when practitioners use an interview guide, they prepare for the possibility that the answers will range across the topics listed in the guide. During the interview they record the responses in the order given. Afterward they can reorganize them according to the topics in the guide.

Questionnaires

Some standardized questionnaires include reliable, structured measures of external relations. These measures can facilitate comparisons between units within a large organization but they cannot not provide the wealth of data obtainable through interviews tailored to the client organization. The International Organizational Observatory (Appendix B) includes useful standardized, open-ended questions that can be administered to managers of both local and multinational firms. This instrument covers topics including interorganizational linkages (e.g., joint ventures, licensing, franchising), anticipated external developments and responses, the firm's overall competitive position, and its position on major products (e.g., major competitors, match between expectations and experience in launching new products). Other instruments cover topics such as environmental predictability (Lawrence & Lorsch, 1969, pp. 247-250; Van de Ven & Ferry, 1980, pp. 241-258) and dependence on external organizations (Gresov, 1989). Many of the items included in the Organizational Assessment Inventory (Van de Ven & Ferry, 1980; Appendix B) apply to both for-profit and not-for-profit organizations.

Analysis and Feedback

Data Analysis and Interpretation

The organization design models presented in chapter 4 can guide an analysis of fits between external conditions and a client organization's structure, technology, and processes. In particular, practitioners can assess whether coordination mechanisms are appropriate to the degree of environmental predictability. Units that face very unpredictable environments or poorly understood conditions (e.g., scientific knowledge about the common cold) will usually need to make more use of complex, lateral coordination mechanisms and organic administrative systems.

Another approach involves examining the uses and consequences of each of the tactics listed in guideline #7. In this way consultants can uncover ways to make current tactics more effective and discover neglected possibilities for managing external relations. An additional procedure for mapping external contacts is described in Exercise 1 below.

Except in very small organizations, each unit in a client organization will deal with a different subenvironment consisting of those sectors of the environment most relevant to the unit's operations. To analyze environmental relations in complex organizations, practitioners need to construct profiles of the main features of the subenvironments of major units. These profiles could note the following features:

- Predictability
- Complexity (number of relevant external organizations and degree of difference between them)
- Competitiveness, dependence on other organizations
- Degree of economic and political threat or support to unit and the organization as whole
- Distinctive problems and challenges posed
- Tactics for managing external relations

To make characterizations of the environments faced by an entire organization or division, practitioners will often have to create a composite picture drawn from the reports of people who are knowledgeable about particular subenvironments. In like manner, practitioners can synthesize data from subunits to assess organization-wide impacts of tactics for managing external relations. To decide which responses to the environment work best, practitioners can compare past responses to current ones or contrast the approaches of units facing similar conditions.

Preparations for Feedback

Feedback of data on environmental relations can focus directly on the effectiveness of current tactics for managing these relations and ways to enhance effectiveness. Alternatively, practitioners can present the findings on the state of the environment and external relations as stimuli for self-analysis and decision making.

In preparing the data for analysis and feedback, consultants should examine how the members of the client organization are reading external conditions and interpreting important environmental developments (Weitzel & Jonsson, 1991). Interpretations of the environment are shaped by many factors, including the members' position in the organization, their work experience and training, their social and cultural backgrounds, their personalities, and the organizational culture. Sometimes members of an organization systematically deny or ignore developments such as client dissatisfaction or sectoral trends, that the consultant and other outsiders such as industry experts regard as critical. Judicious feedback about gaps between internal and external views of the organization can help members become aware of how others view them and can motivate them to take action to improve external relations.

Potential Pitfalls

Although the approach to diagnosing external relations described so far can yield useful findings and recommendations, it has several potential pitfalls. First, it encourages the consultants to draw most of the conclusions about the management of external relations on their own. To develop practical recommendations for improving external relations, practitioners need to listen carefully to the members of the organization who will be responsible for implementing these steps. Involving members in the process of interpreting the diagnostic findings and formulating recommendations may enhance the chances of formulating a workable set of recommendations. Second, the approach described above is very time consuming and costly, since only highly skilled interviewers and analysts can gather and interpret the necessary information. Third, the findings in such a study may not seem valid to clients because the data and interpretations do not sufficiently reflect the clients' own experiences and points of view. Fourth, a consultant-centered analysis of external relations may founder on divergences in members' interests and goals. The diagnosis of external relations often raises questions about the appropriateness of current strategies and tactics for managing external relations. Unless clients can agree on goals and strategies, they are likely to disagree about the steps to take in light of the diagnostic findings and recommendations.

OPEN SYSTEMS PLANNING

Open Systems Planning (OSP) (Beckhard & Harris, 1977, pp. 58-69; Burke, 1982, pp. 65-70; Jayaram, 1976; Fry, 1982) is a client-centered, diagnostic intervention that may help consultants overcome some of the limitations of a consultant-centered diagnosis of external relations. In OSP consultants conduct a series of workshops with members of an organization or subunit who have responsibility and authority to engage in planning and to make decisions affecting the organization's strategic relations to its environment. Workshop participants diagnose their organization's current situation and decide what steps to take to deal with external challenges. The consultant facilitates and guides the discussion, records and summarizes them, and gives feedback without dictating the content of the diagnosis and the planning. Groups whose members are familiar with the background and approach of OSP can also use it without the aid of an external consultant. The following summary of the main steps in OSP includes instructions to participants in the planning process.[1]

1. *Analyze current environmental conditions.* Create a map of the external conditions, groups, and organizations in the task environment and the demands, problems, and opportunities created by these forces.
2. *Analyze current responses to the environment.* Describe the ways that the organization handles these environmental demands and conditions. Consider all important transactions with the task environment.
3. *Analyze actual priorities and purposes.* Define current goals, values, and priorities by examining current responses to the environment and the organization's internal features (structure, processes, culture, etc.). If possible, reach agreement on the organization's guiding mission.
4. *Predict trends and conditions.* Predict likely changes in external conditions over the next 2 to 5 years. Assess the future of the organization if it maintains its current responses to the environment.
5. *Define an ideal future.* Create scenarios for an ideal future state which can envision changes in the organizational purposes and priorities, external conditions, and responses to the environment.
6. *Compare current and ideal states.* In light of projected trends (step 4), define gaps between current and ideal future states in purposes, external conditions, and organizational responses. These gaps may be thought of as differences between where the organization seems to be going and where you want it to go.
7. *Establish priorities.* Assign priorities to the gaps between ideal and current conditions. Define areas of working agreement and identify disagreements about values, priorities, and purposes.
8. *Plan appropriate action.* Plan ways of moving toward agreed-upon future states by narrowing the most important gaps identified in stages 6 and 7. Plan immediate actions and those to be undertaken after 6 months and after 2 years. Consider actions for resolving disagreements. Create a schedule for following up on actions and updating plans.

---

1. This summary, which synthesizes and slightly adapts Jayaram's (1976) approach, also draws on Burke (1982, p. 66) and Plovnick, Fry, and Burke (1982, pp. 69-70). The main advantages of Jayaram's approach over that of Beckhard and Harris (1977, pp. 58-69) is that it allows the definitions of purposes and priorities to emerge from the discussions of the current and ideal states and requires only the achievement of working agreements about operating priorities. This approach to defining goals and priorities seems more realistic than expecting participants to agree in advance on the organization's core mission (see Fry, 1982).

OSP requires participants to use constructive problem-solving techniques to discover and deal with differences in their priorities and objectives. As Jayaram notes, this approach works well only where members trust and cooperate with one another. If participants can reach a working consensus on ideal future states, they may be able to use OSP successfully to assess the organization's current strategic stance toward its environment and to plan changes in this stance (see Beckhard & Harris, 1977, for examples). In addition, to use OSP effectively, participants must have the power to put their plans into action. Otherwise the whole process will become exercise in frustration that may alienate and embitter participants. To conduct OSP, consultants need to be highly skilled in working with groups in training situations as well as have diagnostic skills.

EXERCISES

1. External Contacts

Based on information gathered in previous exercises or in your own involvement in an organization, choose a unit within an organization that has substantial external contacts (both within and beyond the organization's boundaries). Interview the head of the unit using parts IV and V of the General Orientation Interview. Make a chart showing the focal unit at the center and the other units and groups around it. Then color code the chart to show the external groups or units on which the focal unit is most dependent for resources or services, the ones with which contact is most frequent, and any outside units that have authority over the focal unit. Describe the routines and procedures linking the focal unit to two of the most important external units and indicate how these procedures could be improved or how relations with these important units could be improved through other means. (For additional exercises see Lauffer, 1982, pp. 30-42, 1984, pp. 84-87.)

2. Diagnosing External Relations

Construct a detailed interview guide that reflects the issues raised in the Guidelines for Diagnosis given above. Using this guide, interview the head of a unit or small organization. Organize the responses to the interview and your conclusions about it in terms of the categories given in the Guidelines.

6

Challenges and Dilemmas of Diagnosis[1]

Successful diagnosis requires practitioners to meet the requirements of diagnostic process, interpretation, and methods and to achieve a good balance between their responses to each of these challenges. In addition, practitioners must make hard choices concerning project goals, the groups and individuals who are to benefit from diagnosis, and professional standards and personal values and interests. These choices are presented in terms of three diagnostic dilemmas. Practitioners may enhance their chances of conducting useful and influential diagnoses by confronting these dilemmas and working with their clients to resolve them in practical and mutually acceptable ways.

During organizational diagnosis, behavioral science consultants identify problems and opportunities facing their client organizations and help them to chart routes toward enhancing organizational effectiveness. To conduct successful diagnoses, consultants must meet the challenges posed by three facets of diagnosis and achieve a good balance between their responses to each of these challenges. The *processual* challenge requires constructive management of interactions with clients and other organizational stakeholders. The *methodological* challenge is to use the most rigorous and valid techniques for gathering, summarizing, and analyzing data within the constraints imposed by the consulting assignment. The *interpretive* challenge is to use research-based models to identify sources of effectiveness and ineffectiveness and routes toward organizational improvement.

Despite their usefulness, the models discussed in this book and others like them cannot serve as step-by-step guides to diagnosis. Nor can they be used like equations into which bits of data can be inserted to produce a completed assessment. No such recipes for diagnosis or action planning exist and none is likely to be discovered. Instead, most models work best as accounting schemes and guides to help both experienced and beginning practitioners sort out what is going on within an organi-

1. Portions of this chapter draw upon Harrison (1990) and are reproduced with permission of *The Journal of Management Consultation.*

zation. A further limitation of these models is their selective emphasis on particular organizational phenomena. Some focus mainly on one level of analysis and all stress certain organizational features more than others. Only by combining these partial views and shifting between them can practitioners deal with the multifaceted nature of modern organizations (Morgan, 1986).

Anyone who undertakes a diagnosis thus faces many choices about which models and methods to use and how to manage the consulting process. In most cases each alternative has some advantages and some drawbacks. Frequently, the emerging relations between clients and practitioners and practical considerations, such as the accessibility of data, shape the choices among alternatives. Beginning practitioners will need firsthand experience in diagnosis and consulting processes and further training in organizational analysis and research methods to develop the ability to make these judgments themselves.

This chapter locates the immediate choices facing practitioners within the broader context of three types of dilemmas:

- *The Goals Dilemma*—pursuing modest objectives that can be obtained quickly and easily versus pursuing ambitious objectives that require more effort and are riskier.
- *The Politics Dilemma*—seeking benefits for all members of the client organization versus providing selective benefits.
- *The Professionalism Dilemma*—maintaining strict professional standards versus responding to personal needs and interests.

These dilemmas capture central issues facing practitioners and their clients as they negotiate over the nature of a diagnostic project. Although the dilemmas confront practitioners whose interventions in the client organization go beyond diagnosis, this chapter concentrates on the implications for diagnostic work.

By considering these dilemmas before beginning a project, practitioners may be better equipped to handle their emerging relations with clients. As they negotiate with clients, practitioners will need to find ways to raise and clarify the issues highlighted by the diagnostic dilemmas to ensure mutually compatible expectations for the diagnosis. These dilemmas can only be resolved provisionally and partially. Hence consultants will need to reconsider them as the diagnostic project unfolds and changes occur in their needs and expectations and in those of their clients.

THE GOALS DILEMMA

Hierarchy of Goals

Expanding on Turner's (1982) analysis of consulting goals, we can distinguish among the following hierarchy of possible goals for diagnostic studies:

1. *Provide specific information or evaluation*—for example, assessing public satisfaction with automatic teller machines or evaluating whether daycare programs enable mothers to take full-time jobs.
2. *Solve a specific problem*—for example, find ways to reduce employee turnover or improve public satisfaction with an organization's services.
3. *Assess organizational effectiveness and recommend ways to improve effectiveness.*
4. *Contribute to organizational learning*—by helping members of the client organization enhance their capacities to handle problems and challenges and build these enhanced capacities into organizational processes, structures, and culture.
5. *Contribute to organizational transformation*—by helping top management make fundamental changes in key system features, including goals and strategies, structures, processes, technology, and culture.

The first two goals focus on short-term, incremental improvements, while the fourth and fifth goals envision long-term, fundamental impacts. Depending on the effectiveness criteria used, the third goal may aim at either incremental or fundamental, strategic improvements. Practitioners can usually achieve the objectives implied by the first two goals through routine diagnostic work—provided that the information needs or problems fall within their areas of expertise. In contrast, achieving the more ambitious, higher level goals requires greater investments of time and effort by both clients and consultants and is riskier.

Sources of Tension and Conflict

There are at least three sources of the goals dilemma: (1) potential incompatibilities among goals; (2) divergences in goal preferences within the client organization or between clients and consultants; (3) tensions between incentives and disincentives to pursue higher level goals.

Conflicting Goals

Conflicts or tensions between goals arise because the successful achievement of a goal at any given level in the goals hierarchy may block pursuit of a goal at a different level in the hierarchy. For instance, practitioners who accept their clients' definitions of the information needs or problems facing an organization and agree to pursue a very narrow and modest diagnostic goal may find themselves focusing their attention on the symptoms of underlying sources of ineffectiveness, while neglecting these underlying causes. High turnover, for example, may reflect a wide range of underlying problems—including poor interpersonal relations, lack of challenge or room for initiative, and internal conflict—as well as more obvious weaknesses in reward systems or opportunities for advancement.

Likewise, systematically pursuing the goal of improving effectiveness may actually block the consultant's ability to contribute to organizational learning. Consider, for example, the consultant who recommends sophisticated changes in organizational design to encourage innovativeness. Although these changes may enhance current effectiveness, they will not necessarily empower members of the organization to design and implement the next generation of needed design changes on their own. On the contrary, the sophistication of the consultant's recommendations may increase the clients' dependence on outside expertise. In short, pursuit of a lower level goal may undercut the achievement of a higher level one. Moreover, the pursuit of higher level ends may also lead practitioners to neglect the clients' more immediate objectives and thus fail to meet their expectations.

A further source of incompatibility among these goals lies in the tendency for clients and other influential members of the focal organization to type consultants in terms of particular project objectives and intervention styles. Suppose, for example, that a consultant's first project with a client group involves gathering data on the attitudes of managers toward relocating geographically and recommending appropriate incentives for relocation. Once the project becomes known within the organization, its members may associate the consultant with that type of detailed fact-finding and problem solving, and may, therefore, assume that the consultant is not capable of conducting broader projects that have higher level objectives.

Disagreement About Goals

The second source of the goals dilemma lies in gaps between consultants' goal preferences and those of their clients and in gaps among goals held by various members of the client organization. Clients often prefer lower level goals because they promise concrete results with limited costs. In contrast, consultants often aim for higher level goals because projects directed to these goals are longer, more labor intensive, and more lucrative. In addition, pursuit of higher level goals offers consultants the possibility of making a major contribution to a client organization and is often more professionally challenging than handling routine assignments. Hence, consultants may feel torn between pressing for the pursuit of higher level goals and satisfying the expectations of clients who want immediate, certain results.

Disagreement about project goals among powerful stakeholders within and outside the client organization may also occur since the potential risks and benefits of pursuing any particular project goal are not shared equally. For instance, the management of a large division might call on internal consultants to assess the overall operations of one of their units. But the heads of that unit may press for a narrower definition of the study's goals to reduce the threat of negative findings.

Costs Versus Benefits

Third, the goals dilemma stems from the tension between the substantial benefits that both clients and consultants may gain from pursuing higher level goals and the costs and risks to both clients and consultants of pursuing these goals. Understandably, clients often express concerns about the costs and possible risks of entering into expensive, time-consuming projects that may show few results. Clients are likely to be hesitant to enter into studies aimed at improving overall effectiveness or enhancing learning because these ambitious projects require greater client commitment than narrowly focused investigations and are more likely to reveal weaknesses within the top levels of management.

Despite the professional and financial appeals of ambitious projects, consultants also face deterrents to pursuing higher level diagnostic goals. For instance, working toward higher level goals requires the consultant to be more skilled in managing the consulting process. Moreover, many structural, interpersonal, and psychological forces may prevent members of an organization from unlearning ingrained habits and approaches and replacing these habits with alternative ways of thinking and acting. In fact, fundamental reworkings of organizational culture are not often achieved unless the organization has undergone a major crisis or new leaders emerge or are imposed within top management. For these reasons, pursuing higher level goals exposes consultants to greater risks of client dissatisfaction and of project failure than does the pursuit of lower level goals.

Partial Resolutions

Although there is no simple solution to the goals dilemma, several partial resolutions are possible. One popular approach is to begin a project by pursuing lower level diagnostic goals and to define higher level goals only after early successes. This technique of sequencing goals can help consultants and clients pursue what would otherwise be incompatible goals, provided that consultants can avoid being typed as capable of handling only lower level objectives. Sequencing may also help reduce the risks associated with pursuing higher level goals. Moving from lower to higher level goals can build trust between consultants and clients, enhance the consultants' knowledge of the organization before ambitious projects are planned, and enhance the motivation and skills that clients need to pursue difficult projects.

Divergences between goal preferences within the client organization can also be provisionally resolved. When consultants discover such divergences, they can provide feedback on these goal conflicts to clients and request that they reach a working agreement on the study's objectives and priorities before the diagnosis proceeds further. Sequencing diagnostic projects can also help reduce goal divergences within the organization or between clients and consultants, since members of the client organization can usually reach agreement more readily concerning the pursuit of more modest objectives. The multiconstituency approach (chapter 2) suggests another possibility: conducting the diagnosis to mirror the major lines of disagreement among the organization's stakeholders.

THE POLITICS DILEMMA

Who Benefits?[2]

Who is to benefit from the diagnostic study—the client who originally sponsored the study; a particular organizational stratum such as top management; all the members of a unit or group whose problem was

2. The following discussion of the politics and professionalism dilemmas draws in part on Walton and Warwick (1973). For other discussions of professional ethics see Gellerman, Frankel, and Ladenson (1990) and O'Connor (1977).

originally presented to the consultant; or the entire organization? This question captures the essence of the politics dilemma: What range of interests should the diagnosis serve? No matter how cooperative and consensual the relations within an organization, some groups and individuals will benefit more than others from a diagnostic study, and some may suffer in consequence of it.

The most obvious reason that diagnosis may threaten some people is that it may point to weaknesses in their performance. In addition, diagnostic recommendations may suggest enhancing the resources or authority of particular individuals or units. Diagnosis can also have a differential impact on particular members or units, because the process of providing people with additional information and understanding about their organization's operations may increase their power or their ability to take particular actions. There may also be hidden power implications in the ways in which clients and practitioners define problems and selectively focus on some organizational levels or features—for example, labor costs among lower level employees as opposed to managerial practices and organization designs that generate hidden costs and reduce productivity.

Diagnostic recommendations may also support particular value positions at the expense of others. For instance, if consultants recommend that managers delegate more authority and increase participation in decision making, these recommendations may clash with the values and interests of managers who benefit personally from the current concentration of power. It should come as no surprise, then, that people who sense that they stand to gain from a diagnosis will applaud and support the decision to conduct the study, whereas those who expect to lose may oppose it or cooperate only reluctantly. Consultants must therefore decide who are to be the main beneficiaries of their work and what their stance will be toward members who may be threatened by the diagnosis.

Some Solutions

A wide variety of partial resolutions to the politics dilemma is possible. These resolutions range from the pole of seeking to provide benefits to all members of an organization to that of treating the diagnosis as a service to the specific clients who called for the study. According to the former view, which dominated much of the early organization development literature (see chapter 1), consultants are obligated to strive for the improvement of the organization as a whole, not to enhance the position of individuals within it. The goals of diagnosis and intervention are therefore defined as the ultimate improvement of organizational properties such as health, effectiveness, or cohesion. This attempt to benefit all members of the client organization may be criticized for overlooking the realities of power and politics. By focusing on abstract organizational states, consultants may overlook the concrete relations among the people who are affected by the diagnosis. Moreover, practitioners who focus mainly on abstract organizational states may give themselves so much freedom to define what is good for the organization that they end up working for project goals or making recommendations that are not widely understood or accepted within the organization.

Although there are limitations to focusing on overall organizational states, this approach does give added significance to two ethical mandates that apply to practitioners of diagnosis as well as other consultants, no matter how they solve the politics dilemma: First is the consultant's responsibility to preserve the confidentiality of information about individual members of the organization. The second involves avoiding unjustifiable harm to the interests of individual members of the client organization. When consultants seek to produce benefits for the entire organization, these two responsibilities become practical necessities as well as ethical obligations. If diagnosis is justified by its contribution to the organization as a whole, consultants should avoid diagnosing the performance of specific individuals within the organization and should concentrate on assessing the performance of entire organizational units. From this perspective, practitioners should not make recommendations concerning the hiring, placement, or retention of individuals; nor should they report findings about specific people. Moreover, practitioners should make every effort to ensure that none of the data is used in such a way to expose the opinions or actions of individual members. By avoiding the assessment and exposure of individual members, consultants can increase trust and cooperation with the diagnosis and can enhance their ability to contribute to organizational, as opposed to individual-level, change. Unfortunately, this approach often cannot be applied to heads of units, who are closely identified with their unit's operations and held responsible for its performance by management or outside bodies.

Some practitioners favor a resolution of the politics dilemma that is diametrically opposed to the one just presented. This opposing approach argues that practitioners of diagnosis, like other consultants, owe their loyalties primarily to their clients. This resolution has the advantage of removing consultants from involvement in political processes that are beyond their control. Moreover, this resolution can simplify the process of defining project goals and priorities. But it may also suffer from ethical limitations and be unworkable. In practice, it is often very hard to determine the client to whom the consultant owes loyalty. Is it the person who authorized payment for the study, the individual who first asked for it, those who approved and sponsored it, or those who will receive the feedback and act on it? In many cases, these are different people, with divergent needs and interests.

The preceding two resolutions come close to asserting that the solution to the politics dilemma lies in embracing one of the horns of the dilemma: The first approach argues for trying to benefit nearly everyone, while the second implies working for the benefit of a specific individual or subgroup. Other partial resolutions seek to chart a middle course between these two poles by coping realistically and directly with the essentially political character of organizations.

One alternative is to seek broad sponsorship and supervision for the diagnosis, so that members of the organization take on the responsibility for negotiating and resolving many of the power implications of the study. In the Michigan Quality of Work Life project, for example, consultants worked with a committee composed of representatives of management and labor (Mirvis & Seashore, 1980). This committee was responsible for reviewing problems and change opportunities and for initiating actions and solutions. The major drawback of broad sponsorship and supervision of the diagnosis is that it renders the design and interpretation of the study vulnerable to the very political pressures that sponsorship is supposed to overcome.

Bowen (1977) has suggested another way of relieving consultants of the responsibility for solving both the politics and the goals dilemmas. Following Argyris (1970), he argues that the main obligation of consultants is to provide clients with valid information and to allow them the freedom to decide whether and how to act upon this information. This approach has the virtue of discouraging consultants from trying to impose their values and recommendations on the client organization and of encouraging them to accept the fact that the power and responsibility for acting on diagnostic findings lie with members of the organization and not with the consultant. On the other hand, neither Bowen nor Argyris specifies sufficiently what constitutes valid information or who the real clients are. This approach may therefore encourage consultants to underestimate the political impacts of their work and lead them to blame clients for failure to enact recommendations.

A less elegant but more realistic resolution of the politics dilemma begins with the assumption that consultants are responsible to a limited number of clients and that these clients need to define a clear set of expectations and priorities for the diagnosis. A first step, therefore, is to require clients, with or without the aid of the consultant, to define the goals for the study and the evaluative criteria to be used, such as the criteria for assessing organizational effectiveness. Next, practitioners can introduce additional criteria that are compatible with client goals and standards. In addition, practitioners may favor problem definitions and solutions that benefit the widest possible range of groups and individuals but fall within the boundaries set by client priorities.

According to this approach, consultants may advocate particular goals and effectiveness criteria and may favor particular solutions to organizational problems. On the other hand, consultants are restricted to positions compatible with client needs and expectations. Moreover, the final responsibility for interpreting and acting on diagnostic findings lies with the client. A major drawback of this approach is that it can encourage consultants to gear their work too closely to clients' expectations rather than making a comprehensive and objective assessment of the needs of the client organization. In consequence, practitioners may fail to discover sources of ineffectiveness and routes to organizational improvement besides those their clients have already considered. An additional drawback is that consultants may have to choose among several individuals who assert that they are the "real clients" or among several people who perform part of the role of client.

How, then, should consultants decide who is the appropriate client? One answer is that they should look for a person who has both the authority and the expertise needed to use the diagnosis as a means to organizational improvement. From this standpoint the ideal client is often the highest executive officer concerned with the operations of the unit under study—usually the CEO or the head of a semiautonomous division. Another possibility is that the ideal client is the head of a functional department such as Human Resources and is assigned responsibility for handling the challenges and problems being examined by the diagnosis.

This way of defining the client helps practitioners decide with whom they should try to work closely in planning a diagnosis and making recommendations. On the other hand, practitioners may not know at the outset of a project whether particular functionaries have the power and expertise to interpret diagnostic feedback and implement recommendations successfully. Moreover, this approach requires practitioners to make the strong assumption that their clients can define clear, overriding organizational interests or goals and will act on them. A further difficulty is that this solution to the politics dilemma effectively excludes subordinate groups such as labor from participating directly in the definition of project goals or the development of recommendations for action.

In practice, some individuals and groups will usually gain from diagnosis and subsequent changes, while others will lose. Hence, consultants and their clients need to confront the politics dilemma to chart a mutually acceptable course of action. If practitioners anticipate the political impacts of their work, they may be able to reduce the risk that opposition will undermine the study or prevent the implementation of its recommendations.

THE PROFESSIONALISM DILEMMA

This dilemma relates to tensions between strict professional standards and considerations of personal values or self-interest.

Professional Standards Versus Practitioner Interests

One expression of this dilemma is the tension between the dictates of professional integrity and the practitioner's desire to market his or her services, please the client, and maintain professional credibility. In the extreme, this dilemma can boil down to a choice between working to please the client and conducting an honest assessment of the organization. Sometimes practitioners discover that clients have asked for a diagnosis to obtain expert approval for steps they have already planned. In other instances, clients may want to use the diagnosis to ward off critics by showing that the issues are being studied and may be hostile to negative findings. Clients may also pursue a pet theory about what is really going on in the organization and treat alternative approaches as invalid.

External consultants can sometimes avoid or terminate projects that involve such abuses of diagnostic inquiry. But what are internal consultants who cannot turn down assignments without risking their jobs to do? And what can internal or external practitioners do if they have committed themselves to conduct a diagnosis before they discover that their clients has prejudged the results? In such cases, practitioners can try their best to broaden the approach to the study taken by the client and other members of the organization to promote genuinely *organizational* improvements, rather than serving the client's narrow self-interest.

In other cases, it is even harder for practitioners to resolve the tensions between their self-interest and professional obligations and responsibilities. For instance, should practitioners risk using promising but untested models and techniques when these approaches seem appropriate but may not please the client or produce the desired results? Or should they stick to familiar techniques that will produce quick results and make a good impression on clients without contributing much to organizational improvement? Ideally, in such a situation, the practitioner would explain to the clients that the problems cannot effectively be handled with popular, off-the-shelf techniques, and the clients would accept the risks and uncertainties associated with using a newer approach.

A related problem involves practitioners' concerns that they will seem ignorant and lose assignments if they admit that certain problems lie outside of their areas of specialization. But in fact, many important organizational issues lie far beyond the competencies of consultants trained mainly in the social and behavioral sciences. Consultants are professionally obligated to disclose these limitations to clients.

Conflict between professional integrity and self-interest may also stem from the tentative and ambiguous status of applied social and behavioral sciences. As researchers, practitioners are aware that using a different measurement technique or a slightly different definition of variables might alter the results of a study. They also realize that diagnostic issues can be framed in a variety of ways and that there is more than one plausible interpretation of the state of an organization and ways to improve it. Can consultants explain such ambiguities to members of the client organization without making themselves look amateurish and unprofessional?

The answer to this question depends on the ways that consultants define their relations with clients. If consultants present themselves as science-based experts who possess all the knowledge and the tools needed to find a solution to any organizational problem, they will have difficulty admitting such ambiguities. Instead, they can acknowledge that consulting and management are professions that must cope with high levels of ambiguity and complexity (Weick, 1979). Both managers and consultants can respond to these challenges by continually formulating, checking, and reformulating interpretations and explanations (Schon, 1983). From this vantage point, consultants should encourage clients to confront ambiguities by adopting an experimental attitude—"We seem to have a good understanding of what is causing that problem and some good ideas about what to do about them. Let's try them out to see what will happen."

Experiments of this sort can range from systematic tests of the effects of interventions, to less rigorous pilot projects, to an experimental, hypothesis-testing approach to daily affairs. This experimental attitude is illustrated by the manager who has heard about the benefits of delegating authority and decides to test out the theory by encouraging subordinates to assume greater responsibility. The manager examines the ways that delegation is affecting the subordinates and their relations to the manager. In light of this assessment, the manager adjusts his or her behavior accordingly.

An additional form of tension between professional obligations and personal interests is particularly relevant to diagnostic practitioners. Sometimes practitioners will be tempted to propose more elaborate forms of data gathering and analysis than are strictly needed. They may thereby increase their fees or generate data that can be used in academic research or other consulting projects. In both instances, the same kinds of standards that apply to other consulting professions are appropriate here: Like other professionals, diagnostic practitioners should be encouraged to publish reports of their experiences and findings so long as they do not exploit their clients for this purpose. Likewise, no one would have consultants take vows of poverty before entering the profession. But they cannot legitimately pursue personal gain in ways that harm their clients or generate unjustified, hidden costs.

Evaluating Diagnostic Projects

A second expression of the professionalism dilemma involves the evaluation of diagnostic projects. Ideally, diagnostic studies, like other forms of organizational interventions, should be subject to evaluation. Otherwise, practitioners cannot legitimately claim that their work is scientific, nor can they take steps to improve their work. But in practice there are many practical limitations on project evaluation and feedback. Moreover, in some cases consultants may avoid project evaluation to escape criticism or avoid drawing attention to disappointing project results.

Practitioners often lose contact with their clients after completing a diagnosis. Hence they cannot obtain meaningful feedback on its impacts. Even if they receive feedback, objective assessment of the results of diagnosis and other forms of consultation is often impossible. Diagnosis forms only one link in a complex chain of actions that must be completed if the client organization is to achieve the ultimate goal of the diagnosis.

When it is feasible to evaluate a diagnosis, the evaluative criteria must reflect the goals of the diagnosis and take account of the difficulty of isolating the impact of the diagnosis on the organization. Here are several possible evaluative criteria:

1. The perceived usefulness of diagnostic data and information provided to clients and other members.
2. The extent to which the diagnosis helped clients and members solve specific problems.
3. The contribution of the diagnosis to members' own assessments of their organization's effectiveness.
4. The perceived usefulness of recommendations.
5. The degree of use of the diagnostic feedback in decision making and action planning.
6. The degree to which participation in diagnosis and receipt of diagnostic feedback contributes to the clients' ability to engage in self-assessment, group decision making, and planning in the future.

The task of evaluating a diagnosis is further complicated by the requirement that consultants not reveal privileged information about clients and their organizations. Yet evaluation by outside investigators along with criticism and review by peers are needed for objective evaluation and can greatly contribute to the improvement of diagnostic practice. Practitioners can partially compensate for these weaknesses by conducting their own evaluations. In addition, they may publish accounts of their work in which they disguise the identities of client organizations and deal with the abstract, generic significance of their research and experience (Argyris, 1970).

Preserving Personal Integrity

A third expression of the professional dilemma concerns conflicts between the obligations of practitioners to serve their clients and the practitioners' own personal values and ideals. Diagnostic practitioners, like other professionals, have to develop their own personal standards for deciding whether to accept or decline assignments when conflicts arise between their own values and ethical standards and those embodied in the organization's mission and practices and in its members' behavior. Most consultants would, for example, decline an assignment with a business dominated by organized crime. But ethical issues are rarely so clear cut.

Practitioners should ask themselves, for example, whether from the standpoint of their own values and organizational functioning they want their work to enhance the power of top managers and administrators who are already powerful. Some authors (e.g., Alinsky, 1971; Chesler et al., 1978) have responded to the inequalities of power distribution by advocating the use of behavioral science knowledge to assist less powerful groups, such as tenants' unions and block associations in slums. But these change agents do not usually gain sufficient access to the organizations they want to influence to be able to conduct diagnostic studies. At the very least, practitioners of diagnosis should be aware of the political implications of their work and of their implicit value stances concerning the uses and distribution of power.

CONCLUSION

The success of a diagnosis depends greatly on how practitioners resolve the dilemmas presented here and deal with the interpretive, processual, and methodological challenges posed by diagnosis. Practitioners of diagnosis must engage in an elaborate balancing act. They must balance the needs and desires of their clients against those of other stakeholders in the organization and against their own professional understandings of organizational effectiveness. They must also balance the requirements for valid, believable data and analysis against the constraints placed on their time and resources and against the need to promote cooperation with the diagnosis and responsiveness to its findings.

To engage in diagnosis is to undertake a difficult but exciting and rewarding task: to help people find out what is going on in their organization and why, while engaged in a complex, changing web of relations; to find a way of serving clients who may be ambivalent about receiving help and to deal with people who may be dead set against the project; and to sort among project constraints and our other obligations, values, and professional standards.

Appendix A: General Orientation Interview[1]

The orientation interview provides data on the important features of a department or unit and the main challenges and problems facing it. The numbered sections show the main system features covered and the level of analysis. The interview schedule may be modified for divisions or entire organizations and to fit the client organization and specific diagnostic issues. The choice and wording of questions can also be changed during the interview to allow the interviewer and respondent to move comfortably between topics. An orientation interview can last from 30 minutes to 2 hours. The items with asterisks can be left for subsequent interviews or other forms of data gathering if time is short or respondents seem uncomfortable with sensitive issues.

Before starting, the interviewer should explain that the interview is intended to help the consultant learn about what it is like to work in the unit and explain who is sponsoring the study (e.g., division management, with the approval of the union). The interviewer can explain how the respondent was selected (at random, by recommendation, because of his or her position), and that individual answers are confidential and only general summaries of the results will be revealed.

GENERAL ORIENTATION INTERVIEW

I. The Person and His/Her Job (Individual Level)

1. What do you do here? Please tell me about your past experience in the organization and your current job. (Probe for job title, description of work, department, or unit in which person works, previous positions in organization, time spent in them.)
2. What is it like to work here? (Probe for feelings about work and atmosphere, e.g., fun, frustrating, competitive.)

1. This interview draws in part on Burke (1982, pp. 200-202), Levinson (1972, pp. 527-529), and Nadler (1977, pp. 187-191).

II. Work Roles, Technology, and Outputs (Individual and Group Levels)

1. What tasks does your unit (group/department/division/organization) perform? What are the main techniques and means used to do these things?
2. What are the main outputs of this unit—products, services, ideas? What units in the organization or outside it receive these outputs?
3. How does your job fit into the work done here? With whom do you have to work inside and outside the organization to get things done? How do you communicate with them—informal discussions, meetings, telephone, written reports, computer links, etc.?
*4. What kinds of problems do you have to handle at work? When problems occur, how do you handle them? (Probe for solutions that are well known versus the need to discover solutions.) Do you run into many variations and unexpected situations in your work, or is it fairly similar from day to day?
5. Are there difficulties and barriers to getting the work done here or to doing it the way you'd like?

III. Group Structures and Processes—Controls, Coordinating Mechanisms (Group and Organization Levels)

1. How is the work coordinated within the unit? (Probe for the kinds of controls used, e.g., budgets, direct supervision, quality control, periodic evaluations, MBO, etc.)
2. Are goals and objectives spelled out for your unit? If so, how? (Probe for the specification of targets versus general direction and for the ways in which they are specified.)
*3. How do you know when you have done a job well? (Probe for nature of criteria, type of feedback, and time involved in feedback.)

IV. Environment—Relations to Units Within the Organization (Group and Organization Levels)

1. What other units do you have to work with to get work done? How are contacts with other units coordinated?
2. What kinds of things does your unit need to get from other units—funds, approval for actions, materials, people, information, etc.? How do you get these things?
3. Are relations to other units pretty smooth and trouble free or do uncertainties and problems arise? If so, please describe them.

V. Environment—External Relations (Group and Organization Levels)

1. What kinds of contacts does your unit have with external groups or organizations? (See also question II-2.) In what markets or fields (areas) does your unit work (compete)? What kinds of things do people in your unit need to know about what is going on outside the organization? (Probe for important technological conditions.) How do they find out?
2. What are the main kinds of resources—people, materials, services, funds, and information—that you get from these groups and supply to them? On which groups do you depend the most?
3. Do you run into problems and challenges in obtaining or supplying these resources and in dealing with external groups and conditions? If so, please describe them and explain how you handle them.
4. What are the main needs and expectations of your customers/clients/constituencies? How well do your unit and organization as a whole satisfy these expectations?

VI. Structure (Group and Organization Levels)

1. How is the work in this unit organized and how does the unit fit into the whole organization? (Probe for formal structure, e.g., Who is the head of the unit? To whom does the head report? Who reports to the head? If appropriate, ask respondent to draw an organization chart for the unit and to show its relationship to the rest of the organization.)
2. What are the main rules or procedures in your unit that everyone has to follow? How well do they seem to work?
3. What arrangements exist for taking care of people's health, safety, and retirement needs here?
4. Are there opportunities for obtaining additional skills or training while working here?
5. Is there a union here? If so, what is the climate of union-management relations? How involved is the union in issues other than salary and benefits? (Probe for union involvement in issues such as changes in job titles, work arrangements.)
6. What other (informal) groups exist besides the official unit? (Probe for work teams, cliques, links between and within departments, groups of employees from similar ethnic backgrounds, etc.)

VII. Processes (Group Level)

1. How do the informal groups you mentioned affect the way the work is done here? Do they get along with one another?

*2. Do you feel part of any of these groups? If so, if you came up with a new idea or worked especially hard, how would the other people in your group(s) react?
3. Who is your supervisor—the person directly responsible for your work? How closely do you work with your supervisor? What is it like to work with him/her?
4. What is it like to work with the other people in your unit? (Probe for behavior indicating quality, nature of interpersonal relations, e.g., chat a lot or keep to themselves; help one another out.)
5. How do people find out about what's going on in the unit and in the organization as a whole? (Probe for informal and official communication channels and their uses.)
6. How are decisions made in your unit? What about the organization/division as a whole—how are the decisions made that affect your unit?
*7. How much say do you have in decisions affecting your work? To what extent does your supervisor consider your opinions or consult you when making decisions that affect you? (Probe for variations by types of decisions.)
*8. Who are the really influential people in your unit? Who really controls what goes on in the organization as a whole?
9. What do you have to do to get ahead around here? Do you get rewarded for doing your job well? (Probe for kinds of rewards—pay, promotion, praise, feelings of doing well—and the kinds of behavior rewarded in the unit and the organization.)
10. When people in the unit disagree about things, how are these differences resolved? (For example, the boss decides alone; we discuss all the sides of the question until we have the best solution; we compromise, etc.)

VIII. Culture and Processes (Group and Organization Levels)

1. If you were telling a friend what it was really like to work here, how would you describe the atmosphere? (Probe for norms, beliefs about the nature of the work, how it should be done, and employee's involvement in work.)
2. What aspects of work are most emphasized here—(quality, costs, speed, quantity, innovation, etc.)?
*3. Does it pay to take risks or stick your neck out in your unit? (Probe for support for initiative, risk taking, attitudes toward criticism.)

IX. Purposes and Culture (Group and Organizational Levels)

*1. Can you give me an example of one of your unit's major successes or achievements? What about failures? (Probe for criteria for deciding that something succeeded or failed and assumptions about causes.)

*2. What would you say is the overall mission or purpose of your organization? (What does your organization say that it stands for?) How does the organization pursue its mission? (Probe for differences between official and actual purposes.)

3. Do you feel that your unit is operating effectively? What do you mean by effective?

X. History of Unit/Organization (Group and Organization Levels)

1. We've talked a lot about the way things are done in your unit. Could you tell me something about how they got this way? How have things changed since this unit got started? (Note timing of changes.)
2. What about the organization as a whole—how has it changed?

XI. Problems and Challenges (Group and Organization Levels)

1. What do you see as the main challenges that will be facing your unit and organization in the next 2 or 3 years? Do you have any suggestions for how to handle them?
2. What do you feel are the main strengths of your unit? What are the strengths of the organization as a whole? What are the main problems in the unit? What are the main problems in the organization (or division) as a whole?
3. What things seem to be most in need of change in your unit? What about in the organization as a whole? (Probe for reasons for mentioning these problems.)

XII. Individual Satisfactions

*1. (If not already evident) In general, how satisfied are you with working here? What things make you feel most satisfied? With what things are you least satisfied?

Appendix B: Standardized Diagnostic Instruments

Unless otherwise noted, the following instruments are based on questionnaires to be distributed to members of an organization or unit. Typically, individual attitudes, beliefs, or descriptions of conditions are averaged to obtain group scores. Technical information (e.g., scale construction, reliability, validity, administration) appears in published sources on the instrument and may also be available from the contacts listed.[1]

Where no contacts are listed, the instrument is not being developed further. Permission to use or reproduce instruments should be obtained from their publishers.

THREE MAJOR INSTRUMENTS

These instruments are long, research-based questionnaires with many subscales. The first two were developed for purely academic purposes but have many diagnostic applications, while the third was designed as an assessment tool. Practitioners may select among these scales or choose items from within scales.

International Organizational Observatory

This recently developed battery of instruments is now in use by a network of researchers throughout Europe. It includes modules on the Company Profile (basic information), Relations With Other Organizations (including strategic alliances), Strategy, Production System, Re-

1. Information and recent papers on the status of instruments between 1991 and 1993 were graciously provided by Clifford Cammann (MOAQ), Timothy Clark, Ralph Kilmann, Willem Mastenbroek, Robert Pritchard, Marshall Sashkin, Joe Spaeth (National Organizations Study), Andrew Van de Ven, and Edie Wessner (Survey of Organizations). In early 1985, information was provided by Stanley Seashore (MOAQ), Andrew Van de Ven (OAI), and J. Richard Hackman (JDS).

search and Development, Organization Structure, Production, Planning and Control Systems, and Personnel/Human Resource Management. The Personnel/HRM module covers policies and employee characteristics. The mainly open-ended questions are directed at the managing director or the manager in charge of each functional area.

Contact: Timothy Clark, School of Management, the Open University, Walton Hall, Milton Keynes, MK7 6AA, Great Britain. FAX 090-865-5898.

Organizational Assessment Inventory (OAI)

OAI (Van de Ven & Ferry, 1980) is a family of questionnaires that provide sophisticated, sometimes complex data at the individual, unit, divisional, and organizational levels (see chapter 3). Recent research based on OAI (summarized by Gresov, 1989) provides substantial evidence for the reliability, construct validity, and predictive validity of scales constructed from OAI items (see also Van de Ven & Walker, 1984, and Van de Ven & Chu, 1989).

Contact: Andrew Van de Ven, 3M Professor of Human Systems Management, Carlson School of Management, University of Minnesota, Minneapolis, MN 55455. E-mail: MAKC@UMINNI.

Michigan Organizational Assessment Questionnaire (MOAQ)

MOAQ (Cammann et al., 1983) covers a wide range of individual, group, and organization-level variables (see chapter 3). See Seashore et al. (1983) for information on other instruments in the Michigan Quality of Work Life Program.

ADDITIONAL INSTRUMENTS

The following listing illustrates the range of available instruments, rather than attempting to be comprehensive. The instruments listed have all been applied in more than one type of organization. Diagnostic instruments can also be tailored to one type of organization, such as schools. One recent example is the Effective School Battery described in Gottfredson (1987).

Survey of Organizations

This machine-scored instrument gathers individual descriptions of organizational climate, supervisory behavior, peer relationships, group processes, satisfaction, and perceived performance. The survey has been revised several times since publication of a major technical manual (Taylor & Bowers, 1972) and a guide to using the instrument in organization development (Hausser, Pecorella, & Wissler, 1975). The instrument relies heavily on Likert's (1967) model of effectiveness, which focuses on internal system states and work group processes.

Contact: Rensis Likert Associates, 3001 State St., 401 Wolverine Tower, Ann Arbor, MI 48108-9990.

National Organizations Study

This research-oriented interview schedule covers many of the topics listed under Basic Organizational Information (chapter 2). Also covered are employee benefits, responsibility for decision making in a variety of human resource areas, formalization of rules and procedures, performance assessments, and environmental conditions.

Contact: Survey Research Laboratory, University of Illinois, 909 W. Oregon St., Urbana, IL 61801.

Kilmann-Saxton Culture-Gap Survey

Respondents describe actual and desired work group norms (see chapters 3 and 4). Yields four scales: task support, task innovation, social relationships, and personal freedom. Closing gaps between actual and desired norms is predicted to improve performance. For validation see Saxton's doctoral dissertation (available from C. Uxyax at the address below) or the reference to it in Rousseau (1990, p. 174).

Contact: Ralph Kilmann, Program in Corporate Culture, Katz Graduate School of Business, University of Pittsburgh, 211 Mervis Hall, Pittsburgh, PA 15260. FAX (412) 648-1693. Distribution: XICOM Inc., Sterling Forest, Tuxedo, NY 10987. FAX (914) 351-4762.

Organizational Practices Survey

Hofstede, Neuijen, Ohayv, & Sanders (1990) distinguished six dimensions of organizational practices, based on descriptions by members of [the place] "where I work." Data are drawn from a survey of members of 20 different units in 10 Dutch and Danish organizations. The dimensions reflect: (1) Process versus Results Orientation, (2) Employee versus Job Orientation (3) Parochial (i.e., local) versus Professional (i.e., cosmopolitan) Orientation, (4) Open versus Closed (i.e., secretive, exclusive) Communication Climate, (5) Loose versus Tight Control, (6) Normative (rule, value oriented) versus Pragmatic Orientation (customer oriented). Like organizational climate studies (Schneider, 1990), the data from the Organizational Practices Survey seem to reflect behavioral manifestations of organizational culture and may be useful in diagnosing the administrative orientations of units or organizations.

Contact: Geert Hofstede, Director, Institute for Research on Intercultural Cooperation (IRIC), University of Limburg, P.O. Box 616, 6200 MD, Maastricht, The Netherlands.

Job Diagnostic Survey (JDS) and the Job Rating Form (JRF)

JDS—available in a short and long form—focuses specifically on job characteristics and their psychological consequences (e.g., satisfaction, meaningfulness of work) (see chapter 3). JRF is a companion measure in which supervisors describe their subordinates' jobs. See Hackman and Oldham (1980) for technical information and a discussion of the use of the instruments in job redesign.

Productivity Measurement and Enhancement System (ProMES)

ProMES is a technique through which members of an organization can develop and measure group productivity. The technique facilitates comparisons across units or aggregation of unit scores into organization-wide scores (Pritchard, Jones, Roth, Stuebing, & Ekeberg, 1989). Feedback serves as a catalyst for productivity enhancement (Pritchard, Weiss, Goode, & Jensen, 1990). The technique would appear most useful where there are high levels of agreement about unit and organizational goals and procedures and where the desired unit outcomes can be readily defined and measured.

Contact: Robert Pritchard, Director, Industrial/Organizational Psychology Program, Department of Psychology, Texas A & M University, College Station, TX 77843-4235.

Customer-Supplier Quality Scales

Kerklaan (1991) describes ways of assessing key links between customers and suppliers in and outside of the organization. He provides open-ended questions that can be used in quality management audits or as a guide to workshops aimed at defining quality and developing quality improvement plans.

Contact: Willem Mastenbroek, Holland Consulting Group, Sophialaan 19, 1075 BL, Amsterdam, The Netherlands. FAX 020-699-6601.

Leadership Behavior Questionnaire (LBQ)

Ten 5-item scales distinguish the extent to which high-level executives use transactional leadership (i.e., results-oriented management) versus transformational leadership (i.e., using power to empower others to realize the leader's organizational vision) (Sashkin and Burke, 1990). Applicable to both public- and private-sector organizations, the scales have been shown to be correlated with a range of measures of organizational effectiveness.

Contact: Dr. Marshall Sashkin, Office of Educational Research and Improvement, U.S. Department of Education, Washington, DC 20208-5644.

Additional instruments

Many more scales and instruments are described in British Telecom (1984), Cook et al., (1981), Price and Mueller (1986), and Rousseau (1990). The annual *Developing Human Resources* (Pfeiffer, 1993; Appendix D) routinely lists diagnostic instruments. Many are short questionnaires for workshops and team building. University Associates (Appendix D) publishes a wide range of materials on organization development and human resource development, including a variety of instruments for assessment and feedback. Articles in academic journals (see Appendix D) often include or describe instruments for diagnosis.

Appendix C: A Guide to Diagnosing Behavior During Meetings

Unlike previous guides to observing and diagnosing group functioning (e.g., Benne and Sheats, 1948; Schein, 1969), the current guide does not assume an optimal model for group processes. Instead, it recognizes that the features contributing to group effectiveness depend on many variables, including the effectiveness criterion, the task, the organizational context, and the membership of the group (Alderfer, 1977; Porras & Berg, 1978; G. Strauss, 1976). Hence the questions that follow direct attention to important group processes while allowing practitioners to draw their own conclusions about the importance and impact of each factor. Since the questions are merely guides to observations, they do not provide instructions about what particular behaviors to note or how to make inferences from them. Thus to answer each of these diagnostic questions, observers must consult their notes on the behavior observed during the meeting (e.g., shouting), decide how much they can generalize from these observations (e.g., members often shout at one another), and make appropriate inferences from the observations (e.g., shouting shows that members take differences of opinion personally). Users are encouraged to select among the questions, to modify them, and to apply them to fit the particular features of the group being observed and incorporate relevant effectiveness criteria. Besides guiding observations, these questions can provide a framework for feedback and could also be used by groups wishing to engage in self-diagnosis.

QUESTIONS ABOUT GROUP MEETINGS

1. Goals, Targets, and Procedures

Are the goals of the meeting or the problems to be dealt with stated in advance? Are clear guidelines given for the time and resources to be devoted toward reaching these ends? Do participants understand and accept the goals and purposes of the meeting and of the group, or do people seem to have different, hidden agendas for the meeting?

2. Participation

Do participants other than the leader share in developing the goals and guidelines for the meeting? Do most people participate, or do a few talk most of the time? How much airing of divergent opinions occurs? Do participants have the time and ability to examine the information they are given? Are they prepared for the discussion?

3. Flow of Information and Ideas

Are there opportunities for the clarification and development of the ideas and proposals presented? Are ideas and proposals adequately summarized so that participants can keep track of their progress? How much does the chair guide and control the discussion? Does the group move easily from one issue to another, or must these shifts be forced on them by the leader or a minority?

4. Problem Solving

Do participants define clearly the problems facing them and search for alternative solutions before making decisions? Do they consider long-term as well as short-term consequences of actions? Do they examine more than one alternative and weigh dissenting opinions seriously—or do participants slip into "groupthink"—where everyone backs one solution without seriously discussing others? Do participants draw on and learn from past experiences? Do they consider new ideas and solutions to problems as well as familiar, time-tested ones?

5. Decision Making

What kinds of procedures do participants use to decide on the various proposals raised—ignoring the proposal, acceptance or rejection by top authorities, decision by a minority of powerful participants, voting, consensus? Do participants seem to accept these methods? Do these methods seem to produce the best decisions? Do important issues go undecided?

6. Conflict

What important conflicts arise during the meeting? How are they handled—by someone forcing a solution, one party backing down, bargaining, or collaboration in finding a mutually satisfying solution? What are the effects of these conflict-management methods (e.g., members seem angry, alienated, anxious to work together)? Do conflicts stimulate thinking and problem solving or disrupt the meeting?

7. Interpersonal Relations and Feelings

How cohesive is the group? Do differences among members interfere with working together? Are there opportunities for enhancing group solidarity? What kinds of verbal and nonverbal behavior provide cues to participants' feelings (e.g., exclamations, tone of voice, posture)? Do members trust one another? Do they listen to one another or interrupt and ignore others? Do they discuss differences of opinion in terms of common standards and values, or do they treat them as personal conflicts? Do they find the meetings satisfying or frustrating?

8. Outcomes

What are the major outcomes of the meeting—solutions, decisions, proposals, ideas, etc.? Are the implications for action spelled out clearly—including responsibilities for executing them, the time allotted for doing so, and the forms of follow-up and evaluation? How satisfied with the outcomes of the meeting are its participants, leaders, and others affected by the group's work? How well do the outcomes meet other relevant effectiveness criteria (e.g., innovativeness, adaptiveness)?

To decide how important each of the listed items is to group functioning and whether a particular feature such as participation in decision making impacts group effectiveness, practitioners will have to define effectiveness criteria and trace the feature's impact on effectiveness. Take the question of whether participants share in developing goals and guidelines for action. If consultants define the satisfactions and feelings of group members as important indicators of effectiveness, participation in goal setting may indeed facilitate effectiveness. But the impacts of sharing in goal setting may depend on the nature and context of the group. Group members who are highly educated and accustomed to having their professional opinions taken seriously will probably resent having goals and procedures imposed on them. In contrast, in organizations with more authoritarian traditions, such as military organizations, participants more readily accept having goals and procedures set for them. Hence their degree of satisfaction with a group may depend more on their group's outputs than on their participation in goal setting.

Appendix D: Where to Get Training and Experience in Organizational Diagnosis

ACADEMIC TRAINING

Social and behavioral science departments of universities and professional schools offer courses on organizations and organizational behavior that can equip students with methods and conceptual frames that are useful in diagnosis as well as a small number of courses on applied research and organization development. Concentrations in organizational behavior are often available in schools of management. Courses in statistics and quantitative research techniques are widely offered, whereas nonquantitative research techniques such as unstructured observation and open interviewing are most often taught in departments of anthropology and sociology.

WORKSHOPS, SEMINARS, AND CONFERENCES

Many universities offer evening courses that are more oriented toward practice than are courses for credit. Workshops, seminars, and conferences are also sponsored by many professional and academic organizations that have sections devoted to organizational studies or applied organizational work—for example, the American Psychological Association, the Academy of Management, and the American Sociological Association. The Organization Development Institute (11234 Walnut Ridge Rd., Chesterland, OH 44026) sponsors local, national, and international conferences. Also of interest are the organizations and periodicals listed by Gellerman et al. (1990, pp. 498-502) that specialize in business and professional ethics. The following organizations offer a wide variety of courses and workshops throughout the United States and Canada in human resource management and development, and in organization development—including training in diagnosis. Their listing here is not intended to apply approval of any specific course or program.

American Management Association, P. O. Box 319, Saranac Lake, NY 12983.

The National Training Laboratories, P.O. Box 9155, Rosslyn Sta., Arlington, VA 22209.

University Associates, Publishers and Consultants, 8517 Production Ave., P.O. Box 26240, San Diego, CA 92126.

Readers may also wish to inquire whether local applied behavioral science consulting firms offer workshops or training programs in organization development and diagnosis. Names of local firms may be obtained from university professors who specialize in organizational research; listings under management consultants in the Yellow Pages; and from listings such as McLean (1989, 1990) or the Organization Development Institute's registry of professionals.

FOR FURTHER READING

Those who want to read further in fields such as organizational behavior, human resource management, diagnosis, and organization development, begin with basic texts (e.g., Bolman & Deal, 1991; Cummings & Huse, 1989; Daft, 1992; Gordon, 1991; Heneman et al., 1989; Morgan, 1986) and handbooks (Craig, 1987; Dunnette & Hough, 1991; Kubr, 1986; Lorsch, 1987) and consult the references in these books. The following periodicals and annuals often provide material of use to practitioners:

ACADEMIC JOURNALS

Academy of Management Journal
Academy of Management Review
Administrative Science Quarterly
Human Resource Management
Journal of Applied Behavioral Science
Journal of Applied Psychology
Personnel Psychology

RESEARCH ANNUALS

Annual Review of Psychology

Annual Review of Sociology

Research in Organizational Behavior

Research in Organizational Change and Development

Research in Sociology of Organizations

MANAGEMENT AND PRACTICE-ORIENTED PERIODICALS

Academy of Management Executive

Annual: Developing Human Resources

Business Week

Fortune

Harvard Business Review

Organizational Dynamics

Sloan Management Review

References

Abrahamsson, B. (1977). *Bureaucracy or participation: The logic of organization.* Beverly Hills, CA: Sage.

Adizes, I. (1988). *Corporate lifecyles: How and why corporations grow and die and what to do about it.* Englewood Cliffs, NJ: Prentice-Hall.

Adler, N., & Bartholomew, S. (1992). Managing globally competent people. *Academy of Management Executive, 6*(3), 52-65.

Alderfer, C. (1977). Organization development. *Annual Review of Psychology, 28,* 197-223.

Alinsky, S. (1971). *Rules for radicals.* New York: Random House/Vintage.

Andrews, K. (1971). *The concept of corporate strategy.* Homewood, IL: Dow-Jones, Irwin.

Argyris, C. (1970). *Intervention theory and method.* Reading, MA: Addison-Wesley.

Argyris, C., & Schon, D. (1978). *Organizational learning: A theory of action perspective.* Reading, MA: Addison-Wesley.

Ashforth, B., & Lee, R. (1990). Defensive behavior in organizations. *Human Relations, 43,* 621-648.

Austin, M. (1982). *Evaluating your agency's programs.* Beverly Hills, CA: Sage.

Bacharach, S. (1989). Organizational theories: Some criteria for evaluation. *Academy of Management Review, 14,* 496-515.

Bartlett, C., & Ghoshal, S. (1990). Matrix management: Not a structure, a frame of mind. *Harvard Business Review, 68*(4), 138-145.

Bartunek, J., & Louis, M. R. (1988). The interplay of organization development and transformation. *Research in Organizational Change and Development, 2,* 97-134.

Bartunek, J., & M. Moch (1987). First-order, second-order, and third-order change and organization development interventions: A cognitive approach. *Journal of Applied Behavioral Science, 23,* 483-500.

Bass, B., & Avolio, B. (1990). The implications of transactional and transformational leadership for individual, team, and organizational development. *Research in Organizational Change and Development, 4,* 231-272.

Beckhard, R. (1969). *Organization development: Strategies and models.* Reading, MA: Addison-Wesley.

Beckhard, R., & Harris, R. (1975). Strategies for large system change. *Sloan Management Review, 16,* 43-55.

Beckhard, R., & Harris, R. (1977). *Organizational transitions: Managing complex change.* Reading, MA: Addison-Wesley.

Beer, M. (1980). *Organizational change and development—A systems view.* Santa Monica, CA: Goodyear.

Beer, M., & Walton, A. E. (1987). Organization change and development. *Annual Review of Psychology, 38,* 339-367.

Benfari, R., & Knox, J. (1991). *Understanding your management style: Beyond the Meyers-Briggs Type Indicators.* Lexington, MA: Lexington Books.

Benne, K., & Sheats, P. (1948). Functional roles of group members. *Journal of Applied Behavioral Science, 13,* 543-556.

Bennis, W., Benne, K., & Chin, R. (Eds.). (1985). *The planning of change* (4th ed.). New York: Holt, Rinehart & Winston.

Blake, R., & Mouton, J. (1964). *The managerial grid.* Houston: Gulf.

Blau, P. (1955). *Dynamics of bureaucracy.* Chicago: University of Chicago Press.

Block, P. (1981). *Flawless consulting.* San Diego, CA: University Associates.

Bolman, L. G., & Deal, T. (1991). *Reframing organizations: Artistry, choice, and leadership.* San Francisco: Jossey-Bass.

Bowditch, J., & Buono, A. (1989). *Quality of work life assessment* (2nd ed.). Boston: Auburn.

Bowen, D. (1977). Value dilemmas in organization development. *Journal of Applied Behavioral Science, 13,* 543-556.

British Telecom (1984). *Survey item bank, vol. 2: Measures of organizational characteristics.* Bradford: MCB University Press.

Bullock, R. J., & Svyantek, D. J. (1987). The impossibility of using random strategies to study the organization development process. *Journal of Applied Behavioral Science, 23,* 255-262.

Bullock, R. J., & Tubbs, M. (1987). The case meta-analysis method for OD. *Research in Organizational Change and Development, 1,* 171-228.

Buono, A. (1991). Managing strategic alliances: Organizational and human resource considerations. *Business in the contemporary world,* (Summer), 92-101.

Buono, A., & Bowditch, J. (1989). *The human side of mergers and acquisitions: Managing collisions between people, cultures, and organizations.* San Francisco: Jossey-Bass.

Buono, A., & Bowditch, J. (1990). Ethical considerations in merger and acquisition management: A human resource perspective. *SAM Advanced Management Journal,* (Autumn), 18-23.

Burke, W. W. (1982). *Organization development.* Boston: Little, Brown.

Burns, T. (1961). Micropolitics: Mechanisms of institutional change. *Administrative Science Quarterly, 6,* 256-281.

Burns, T., & Stalker, G. M. (1961). *The management of innovation.* London: Tavistock.

Business Week. (1981). The new industrial relations. May 11, pp. 85-93.

Cameron, K. (1980). Critical questions in assessing organizational effectiveness. *Organizational Dynamics, 9,* 66-80.

Cameron, K. (1984). The effectiveness of ineffectiveness. *Research in Organizational Behavior, 6,* 235-285.

Cameron, K., Kim, M. U., & Whetten, D. (1987). Organizational effects of decline and turbulence. *Administrative Science Quarterly, 32,* 222-240.

Cameron, K., & Quinn, R. E. (1988). Organizational paradox and transformation. In R. E. Quinn & K. Cameron (Eds.), *Paradox and transformation: Toward a theory of change in organization and management* (pp. 1-18). Cambridge, MA: Ballinger.

Cameron, K., Sutton, R., & Whetten, D. (1988). Issues in organizational decline. In K. Cameron, R. Sutton, & D. Whetten (Eds.) *Readings in organizational decline: Frameworks, research, and prescriptions* (pp. 3-19). Cambridge, MA: Ballinger.

Cammann, C., Fichman, M., Jenkins, G., & Kelsh, J. (1983). Assessing the attitudes and perceptions of members. In S. Seashore et al. (Eds.), *Assessing organizational change* (pp. 71-138). New York: Wiley.

Campbell, D. (1977). On the nature of organizational effectiveness. In P. Goodman & J. Pennings (Eds.), *New perspectives on organizational effectiveness* (pp. 13-55). San Francisco: Jossey-Bass.

Carlisle, H. (1974). A contingency approach to decentralization. *SAM Advanced Management Journal,* (July).

Chesler, M., Crawfoot, J., & Bryant, B. (1978). Power training: An alternative path to conflict management. *California Management Review, 21,* 84-91.

Child, J. (1977). *Organization: A guide to problems and practice.* New York: Harper and Row.

Chin, R., & Benne, K. (1985). General strategies for effecting changes in human systems. In W. Bennis, K. Benne, & R. Chin (Eds.), *The planning of change* (4th ed.) (pp. 22-45). New York: Holt, Rinehart and Winston.

Cobb, A. T. (1986). Political diagnosis: Applications of organizational development. *Academy of Management Review, 11,* 482-497.

Connolly, E., & Deutsch, S. (1980). Organizational effectiveness: A multi-constituency approach. *Academy of Management Review,* 5, 211-218.

Cook, J., Hepworth, S., Wall, T., & Wair, P. (1981). *Experience of work: A compendium and review of 249 measures and their use.* New York: Academic Press.

Cook, T., Campbell, D., & Peracchio, L. (1991). Quasi-experimentation. In H. Dunette, & L. Hough (Eds.), *Handbook of industrial and organizational psychology* (2nd ed.) (vol. 1, pp. 491-576). Palo Alto: Consulting Psychologists' Press.

Coombs, G. (1992). Organizational demography: Implications for the organization development practitioner. *Research in the Sociology of Organization, 10,* 199-220.

Craig, R. (Ed.). (1987). *Training and development handbook: A guide to human resource development* (3rd ed.). New York: McGraw-Hill.

Cranny, C. J., Smith, P., & Stone, E. (Eds.) (1992). *Job satisfaction: How people feel about their jobs and how it affects their performance.* New York: Lexington Books.

Cummings, T., & Huse, E. (1989). *Organization development and change* (3rd ed.). St. Paul, MN: West.

Daft, R. (1992). *Organizations: Theory and design* (4th ed.). St. Paul, MN: West.

Davis, L., & Cherns, A. (1975). *The quality of working life* (Vols. 1 and 2). New York: Free Press.

Davis, S. (1984). *Managing corporate culture.* Cambridge, MA: Ballinger.

Davis, S., & Lawrence, P. with H. Kolodny & M. Beer. (1977). *Matrix.* Reading, MA: Addison-Wesley.

Delbecq, A., & Mills, P. (1985). Managerial practices that enhance innovation. *Organizational Dynamics, 14*(1), 24-34.

Dunnette, H., & Hough, L. (Eds.). (1991). *Handbook of industrial and organizational psychology* (2 vols.), (2nd ed.). Palo Alto: Consulting Psychologists' Press.

Dunphy, D., & Stace, D. (1988). Transformational and coercive strategies for planned organizational change: Beyond the OD model. *Organization Studies, 9,* 317-334.

Dyer, W. (1977). *Team building: Issues and alternatives.* Reading, MA: Addison-Wesley.

Eden, D. (1986). Team development: Quasi-experimental confirmation among combat companies. *Group and Organization Studies, 11,* 33-46.

Eisenhardt, K., & Westcott, B. (1988). Paradoxical demands and the creation of excellence: The case of Just-in-Time manufacturing. In R. E. Quinn & K. Cameron (Eds.), *Paradox and transformation: Toward a theory of change in organization and management* (pp. 169-193). Cambridge, MA: Ballinger.

Enz, C. (1989). The measurement of perceived intraorganizational power: A multi-respondent perspective. *Organization Studies, 10,* 241-251.

Faucheux, C., Amando, G., & Laurent, A. (1982). Organizational development and change. *Annual Review of Psychology, 33,* 343-370.

Fielding, N., & Lee, R. (Eds.). (1992). *Using computers in qualitative research.* London: Sage.

Finkelstein, S. (1992). Power in top management teams: Dimensions, measurement, and validation. *Academy of Management Journal, 35,* 505-538.

Fishbein, M., & Ajzen, I. (1975). *Beliefs, attitudes, intention, and behavior.* Reading, MA: Addison-Wesley.

Fisher, C., & Locke, E. (1992). The new look in job-satisfaction research and theory. In C. J. Cranny, P. Smith, & E. Stone (Eds.), *Job satisfaction: How people feel about their jobs and how it affects their performance* (pp. 165-194). New York: Lexington Books.

Florida, R., & Kenney, M. (1991). The transfer of Japanese industrial organization to the U.S. *American Sociological Review 56,* 381-398.

Fombrun, C., Tichy, N., & DeVanna, M. (Eds.). (1984). *Strategic human resource management.* New York: Wiley.

Ford, J., & Baucus, D. (1987). Organizational adaptation to performance downturns: An interpretation-based perspective. *Academy of Management Review, 12,* 366-380.

Fottler, M. (1981). Is management really generic? *Academy of Management Review, 6,* 1-12.

Fox, A. (1974). *Beyond contract: Work, power and trust relations.* London: Faber and Faber.

Freeman, H., Dynes, R., Rossi, P., & Whyte, W. F. (Eds.) (1983). *Applied sociology.* San Francisco: Jossey-Bass.

Freeman, H., & Rossi, P. (1984). Furthering the applied side of sociology. *American Sociological Review, 49,* 560-585.

French, W., & Bell, C. (1984). *Organization Development* (3rd ed.). Englewood Cliffs, NJ: Prentice-Hall.

Fry, R. (1982). Improving trustee, administrator, and physician collaboration through open systems planning. In M. Plovnick et al. (Eds.), *Organization development: Exercises, cases and readings* (pp. 282-292). Boston: Little, Brown.

Galbraith, J. (1977). *Organization design.* Reading, MA: Addison-Wesley.

Galbraith J., Lawler, E., & Associates. (1993). *Organizing for the future: The new logic for managing complex organizations.* San Francisco: Jossey-Bass.

Gellerman, W., Frankel, M., & Ladenson, R. (1990). *Values and ethics in organization and human systems development.* San Francisco: Jossey-Bass.

Glueck, W. (1982). *Personnel: A Diagnostic Approach* (3rd ed.). Plano, Texas: Business Publications.

Goodman, P. S. (1977). Social comparison processes. In B. Staw & G. Salancik (Eds.), *New directions in organizational behavior.* Chicago: St. Clair.

Goodman, P. S., & Pennings, J. (1980). Critical issues in assessing organizational effectiveness. In E. Lawler et al. (Eds.), *Organizational assessment* (pp. 185-215). New York: Wiley.

Gordon, J. (1991). *A diagnostic approach to organizational behavior* (3rd ed.). Boston: Allyn & Bacon.

Gottfredson, G. (1987). An evaluation of an organization development approach to reducing school disorder. *Evaluation Review, 11,* 739-763.

Gray, B., & Ariss, S. (1985). Politics and strategic change across organizational life cycles. *Academy of Management Review,* 10, 707-723.

Greenbaum, T. (1988). *The practical handbook and guide to focus group research.* Lexington, MA: Heath.

Greenlagh, L. (1982). Organizational decline. *Research in the Sociology of Organizations, 2,* 231-276.

Greenlagh, L. (1986). Managing conflict. *Sloan Management Review, 26* (Summer), 45-51.

Gregory, K. (1983). Native-view paradigms: Multiple cultures and culture conflicts in organizations. *Administrative Science Quarterly, 28,* 359-376.

Greiner, L., & Schein, V. (1988). *Power and organization development : Mobilizing power to implement change.* Reading, MA: Addison-Wesley.

Gresov, C. (1989). Exploring fit and misfit with multiple contingencies. *Administrative Science Quarterly, 34,* 431-453.

Griffen, R. (1988). Consequences of quality circles in an industrial setting: A longitudinal assessment. *Academy of Management Journal, 31,* 338-359.

Griffen, R. (1991). Effects of work redesign on employee perceptions, attitudes, and behaviors: A long-term investigation. *Academy of Management Journal, 34,* 425-435.

Guzzo, R. A., Jackson, S., & Katzell, R. (1987). Meta-analysis analysis. *Research in Organizational Behavior, 9,* 407-442.

Hackman, R., & Oldham, G. (1980). *Work redesign.* Reading, MA: Addison-Wesley.

Hall, R. (1987). *Organizations: Structure, process, and outcomes* (4th ed.). Englewood Cliffs, NJ: Prentice-Hall.

Harrison, M. (1990). Hard choices in diagnosing organizations. *Journal of Management Consulting, 6*(1), 13-21.

Harrison, M. (1991). The politics of consulting for organizational change. *Knowledge and Policy, 4,* 92-107.

Harrison, M., & Phillips, B. (1991). Strategic decision making: An integrative explanation. *Research in the Sociology of Organizations, 9,* 319-358.

Harrison, R. (1970). Choosing the depth of organizational intervention. *Journal of Applied Behavioral Science, 6,* 181-202.

Hausser, C., Pecorella, P., & Wissler, A. (1975). *Survey guided development: A manual for consultants.* Ann Arbor: Institute for Social Research, University of Michigan.

Hayes, R., & Abernathy, W. (1980). Managing our way to economic decline. *Harvard Business Review, 58,* 67-77.

Heneman, H. G., III, Schwab, D., Fossum, J., Dyer, L. (1989). *Personnel/Human Resource Management* (4th ed.). Homewood, IL: Irwin.

Hennestad, B. (1988). Inculture: The organizational culture of INC. In S. Tyson, K. F. Ackermann, M. Domsch, & P. Joynt (Eds.), *Appraising and exploring organisations.* London: Croom Helm.

Hofstede, G., Neuijen, B., Ohayv, D., & Sanders, G. (1990). Measuring organizational cultures: A qualitative and quantitative study across twenty cases. *Administrative Science Quarterly, 35,* 286-316.

Hrebiniak, L. G., & Joyce, W. F. (1985). Organizational adaptation: Strategic choice and environmental determinism. *Administrative Science Quarterly, 30,* 336-349.

Huber, G., Miller, C., & Glick, W. (1991). Developing more encompassing theories about organizations: The centralization-effectiveness relationship as an example. *Organization Science, 1,* 11-40.

Huff, A. (1980). Organizations as political systems: Implications for diagnosis, change, and stability. In T. G. Cummings (Ed.), *Systems theory for organization development* (pp. 163-180). Chichester, Eng.: Wiley.

Ironson, G. (1992). Job stress and health. In C. J. Cranny, P. Smith, & E. Stone (Eds.), *Job satisfaction: How people feel about their jobs and how it affects their performance* (pp. 219-239). New York: Lexington Books.

Izraeli, D. N. (1975). The middle manager and tactics of power expansion—A case study. *Sloan Management Review, 16,* 56-70.

Jaeger, A. (1986). Organization development and national culture: Where's the fit? *Academy of Management Review, 11,* 178-190.

Jamieson, D., & O'Mara, J. (1991). *Managing workforce 2000: Gaining the diversity advantage.* San Francisco: Jossey-Bass.

Jayaram, G. (1976). Open systems planning. In W. Bennis et al. (Eds.), *The planning of change* (3rd ed.) (pp. 275-283). New York: Holt, Rinehart & Winston.

Jick, T. (1979). Mixing qualitative and quantitative methods: Triangulation in action. *Administrative Science Quarterly, 24,* 602-611.

Johnson, R., Hoskisson, R., and Margulies, N. (1990). Corporate restructuring: Implications for organizational change and development. *Research in Organizational Change and Development, 4,* 141-166.

Judd, C., Smith, E., & Kidder, L. (1991). *Research methods in social relations* (6th ed.). New York: Holt, Rinehart, & Winston.

Kakabadse, A., & Parker, C. (Eds.) (1984). *Power politics and organizations:A behavioral science view.* Chichester, Eng.: Wiley.

Kanter, R. (1977). *Men and women of the corporation.* New York: Basic.

Kanter, R. (1979). Power failure in management circuits. *Harvard Business Review, 57,* 65-75.

Kanter, R. (1983). *The change masters: Innovation for productivity in the American corporation.* New York: Simon and Schuster.

Kanter, R., & Brinkerhoff, D. (1981). Organizational performance. *Annual Review of Sociology, 7,* 321-349.

Kanter, R. M., & Summers, D. (1987). Doing well while doing good: Dilemmas of performance measurement in nonprofit organizations and the need for a multiple-constituency approach. In W. Powell (Ed.), *The nonprofit sector: A research handbook* (pp. 154-166). New Haven: Yale University Press.

Katz, D., & Kahn, R. (1978). *The social psychology of organizations* (2nd ed.). New York: Wiley.

Katz, H. C., Kochan, T., & Weber, M. (1985). Assessing the effects of industrial relations systems and efforts to improve the quality of working life on organizational effectiveness. *Academy of Management Journal, 28,* 509-526.

Kerklaan, L. (1991). Diagnosis of quality in service: The quality scales in auditing customer supplier relations. In W. Mastenbroek (Ed.), *Managing for quality in the service sector.* London: Blackwell.

Kets de Vries, M. (1979). Organizational stress: A call for management action. *Sloan Management Review, 21,* 3-14.

Khandwalla, P. (1977). *The design of organizations.* New York: Harcourt, Brace, Jovanovich.

Kidder, T. (1981). *The soul of a new machine.* Boston: Little, Brown.

Kiggundu, M. (1986). Limitations to the application of socio-technical systems in developing countries. *Journal of Applied Behavioral Science, 22,* 341-353.

Kilmann, R., Covin, T., & Associates. (1988). *Corporate transformations: Revitalizing organizations for a competitive world.* San Francisco: Jossey-Bass.

Kilmann, R., & Saxton, M. (1981). *Kilmann-Saxton Culture-Gap Survey.* Tuxedo, NY: Organization Design Consultants (Xicom, Inc., distributors).

Kinnear, T., & Taylor, J. (1987). *Marketing research: An applied approach.* New York: McGraw Hill.

Kolb, D., & Frohman, A. (1970). An organization development approach to consulting. *Sloan Management Review, 12,* 51-65.

Kotter, J., & Heskett, J. (1992). *Corporate culture and performance.* New York: Free Press.

Kotter, J., & Schlesinger, L. (1979). Choosing strategies for change. *Harvard Business Review, 57,* 106-114.

Krantz, J. (1985). Group processes under conditions of organizational decline. *Journal of Applied Behavioral Science, 21,* 1-18.

Kubr, M. (1986). *Management consultation: A guide to the profession.* Geneva: International Labor Office.

Kunda, G. (1992). *Engineering culture: Control and commitment in a high-tech corporation.* Philadelphia: Temple University Press.

Lauffer, A. (1982). *Assessment tools: For practitioners, managers, trainers.* Beverly Hills, CA: Sage.

Lauffer, A. (1984). *Understanding your social agency.* (2nd ed.) Beverly Hills, CA: Sage.

Lawler, E. (1977). Reward systems. In J. Hackman & J. Suttle (Eds.), *Improving life at work: Behavioral science approaches to organizational change* (pp. 166-226). Santa Monica, CA: Goodyear.

Lawler, E. (1986). *High involvement management: Participative strategies for improving organizational performance.* San Francisco: Jossey-Bass.

Lawler, E., & Bacharach, S. (1983). Political action and alignments in organizations. *Research in the Sociology of Organizations, 2,* 83-108.

Lawler, E., & Drexler, J. (1980). Participative research: The subject as co-researcher. In E. Lawler et al. (Eds.), *Organizational assessment* (pp. 535-547). New York: Wiley.

Lawler, E., Nadler, D., & Cammann, C. (Eds.). (1980). *Organizational assessment.* New York: Wiley.

Lawler, E., Nadler, D., & Mirvis, P. (1983). Organizational change and the conduct of organizational research. In S. Seashore et al. (Eds.), *Assessing organizational change* (pp. 19-48). New York: Wiley.

Lawler, E., & Rhode, J. (1976). *Information and control in organizations.* Santa Monica, CA: Goodyear.

Lawrence, P., & Lorsch, J. (1969). *Organization and environment.* Homewood, IL: Irwin.

Leach, J. (1979). The organizational history: A consulting analysis and intervention tool. In G. Gore & R. Wright (Eds.), *The academic consultant connection* (pp. 62-69). Dubuque, IA: Kendall/Hunt.

Levinson, H. (1972). *Organizational diagnosis.* Cambridge: Harvard University Press.

Likert, R. (1967). *The human organization.* New York: McGraw-Hill.

Lofland, J. & Lofland, L. (1984). *Analyzing social settings: A guide to qualitative observation and analysis* (2nd ed.). Belmont, CA: Wadsworth.

Lorsch, J. (Ed.). (1987). *Handbook of organizational behavior.* Englewood Cliffs, NJ: Prentice-Hall.

Lundberg, C. (1990). Innovative organization development procedures. Part II: Surfacing Organizational Culture. *Journal of Managerial Psychology, 5*(4), 19-26.

Majchrzak, A. (1984). *Methods for policy research.* Beverly Hills, CA: Sage.

Manzini, A. (1988). *Organizational diagnosis: A practical approach to company problem solving and growth.* New York: AMACOM.

McCracken, G. (1988). *The long interview.* Newbury Park, CA: Sage.

McGregor, D. (1960). *The human side of enterprise.* New York: McGraw Hill.

McLean, J. (1989). *Consultants and consulting organizations* (10th ed.). Detroit: Gale Research.

McLean, J. (1990). *Training and development organizations directory* (5th ed.). Detroit: Gale Research.

McMahan, G. C., & Woodman, R. W. (1992). The current practice of organization development within the firm: A survey of large industrial corporations. *Group and Organization Management, 117,* 117-134.

Meyer, J., & Rowan, B. (1977). Institutionalized organizations: Formal structure as myth and ceremony. *American Journal of Sociology, 83,* 340-363.

Meyer, M., & Zucker, L. (1989). *Permanently failing organizations.* Newbury Park, CA: Sage.

Miles, M., & Huberman, A. M. (1984). *Qualitative data analysis: A sourcebook of new methods.* Beverly Hills, CA: Sage.

Miles, R. E., & Snow, C. (1978). *Organizational strategy, structure, and process.* New York: McGraw-Hill.

Miles, R. H. (1980). *Macro organizational behavior.* Santa Monica, CA: Goodyear.

Mills, A., & Tancred, P. (Eds.). (1992). *Gendering Organizational Analysis.* Newbury Park, CA: Sage.

Mills, D. Q. (1991). *Rebirth of the corporation.* New York: Wiley.

Mintzberg, H. (1979). *The structuring of organizations.* Englewood Cliffs, NJ: Prentice-Hall.

Mintzberg, H. (1983). *Power in and around organizations.* Englewood Cliffs, NJ: Prentice-Hall.

Mintzberg, H. (1984). Power and organizational life cycles. *Academy of Management Review,* 9, 207-224.

Mirvis, P., & Seashore, S. (1980). Being ethical in organizational research. In E. Lawler et al. (Eds.), *Organizational Assessment* (pp. 583-612). New York: Wiley.

Moch, M., Cammann, C., & Cooke, R. (1983). Organizational structure: Measuring the degree of influence. In S. Seashore et al. (Eds.), *Assessing organizational change* (pp. 177-202). New York: Wiley.

Moch, M., Feather, J., & Fitzgibbons, D. (1983). Conceptualizing and measuring the relational structure of organizations. In S. Seashore et al. (Eds.), *Assessing organizational change* (pp. 203-228). New York: Wiley.

Morgan, G. (1986). *Images of organizations.* Newbury Park, CA: Sage.

Morgan, G. (1988). *Riding the waves of change: Developing managerial competencies for a turbulent world.* San Francisco: Jossey-Bass.

Morton, M. (Ed.). (1991). *The corporation of the 1990's: Information technology and organizational transformation.* New York: Oxford.

Nadler, D. (1977). *Feedback and organization development: Using data-based methods.* Reading, MA: Addison-Wesley.

Nadler, D. (1988). *Organizational frame bending: Types of change in the complex organization.* In R. Kilmann, T. Covin, & Associates, *Corporate transformations: Revitalizing organizations for a competitive world* (pp. 66-83). San Francisco: Jossey-Bass.

Nadler, D., & Lawler, E. (1983). Quality of work life: Perspectives and directions. *Organizational Dynamics, 11,* 20-30.

Nadler, D., Mirvis, P., & Cammann, C. (1976). The ongoing feedback system: Experimenting with a new management tool. *Organizational Dynamics, 4,* 63-80.

Nadler, D., & Tushman, M. (1980a). A congruence model for diagnosing organizational behavior. In E. Lawler et al. (Eds.), *Organizational Assessment* (pp. 261-278). New York: Wiley.

Nadler, D., & Tushman, M. (1980b). A model for diagnosing organizational behavior. *Organizational Dynamics, 9,* 35-51.

Nadler, D., & Tushman, D. (1989). Leadership for organizational change. In A. M. Mohrman, S. A. Mohrman, G. E. Ledford, Jr., T. Cummings, & E. Lawler (Eds.), *Large scale organizational change* (pp. 100-119). San Francisco: Jossey-Bass.

Nees, D., & Greiner, L. (1985). Seeing behind the look-alike management consultants. *Organizational Dynamics, 13,* 68-79.

Nelson, R. E. (1988). Social network analysis as an intervention tool. *Group and Organization Studies , 13,* 39-58.

Newman, W., & Warren, E. (1981). *The process of management* (5th ed.). Englewood Cliffs, NJ: Prentice-Hall.

Newson-Smith, N. (1986). Desk research. In R. Worcester & J. Downham (Eds.), *Consumer market research handbook* (3rd ed.) (pp. 7-27). New York: North Holland.

Nightingale, O., & Toulouse, J. (1977). Toward a multi-level congruence theory of organization. *Administrative Science Quarterly, 22,* 264-280.

O'Connor, P. (1977). A critical inquiry into some assumptions and values characterizing O.D. *Academy of Management Review,* 2, 635-644.

Orton, J. D., & Weick, K. (1990). Loosely coupled systems: A reconceptualization. *Academy of Management Review, 15,* 203-223.

Osborn, R., & Baughn, C. (1993). Societal considerations in the global technological development of economic institutions: The role of strategic alliances. *Research in the Sociology of Organizations,* forthcoming.

Ouchi, W. (1981). *Theory Z: How American business can meet the Japanese challenge.* Reading, MA: Addison-Wesley.

Passmore, W. J., Petee, J., & Bastian, R. (1986). Sociotechnical systems in health care: A field experiment. *Journal of Applied Behavioral Science, 22,* 329-339.

Pennings, J. (1992). Structural contingency theory: A reappraisal. *Research in Organizational Behavior 14,* 267-309.

Perkins, D., Nadler, D., & Hanlon, M. (1981). A method for structured naturalistic observation of organizational behavior. In J. Pfeiffer & J. Jones (Eds.), *The 1981 annual handbook for group facilitators* (pp. 222-244). San Diego, CA: University Associates.

Peters, T., & Waterman, R. (1982). *In search of excellence.* New York: Harper and Row.

Pfeffer, J. (1981a). Management as symbolic action: The creation and management of organizational paradigms. *Research in Organizational Behavior, 3,* 1-52.

Pfeffer, J. (1981b). *Power in organizations.* Marshfield, MA: Pitman.

Pfeffer, J., & Salancik, G. (1978). *The external control of organizations.* New York: Harper and Row.

Pfeiffer, J. (1993). *The 1993 annual: Developing human resources.* San Diego, CA: University Associates.

Phillips, B. (1991). Significant events: An applied sociologist learns to play the corporate game. *Sociological Practice Review, 1,* 59-67.

Plovnick, M., Fry, R., & Burke, W. (1982). *Organization development: Exercises, cases, and readings.* Boston: Little, Brown.

Pondy, L. (1967). Organizational conflict: Concepts and models. *Administrative Science Quarterly, 12,* 296-320.

Porras, J., & Berg, P. (1978). The impact of organizational development. *Academy of Management Review, 3,* 249-266.

Porras, J., & Robertson, P. (1987). Organization development theory: A typology and evaluation. *Research Organizational Change and Development, 1,* 1-57.

Porras, J., & Robertson, P. (1992). Organization development: Theory, research, and practice. In M. Donnette & L. Hough (Eds.), *Handbook of organizational and industrial psychology, Volume 3* (2nd ed.). Palo Alto, CA: Consulting Psychologists Press.

Porras, J., & Silver, R. (1992). Organization development and transformation. *Annual Review of Psychology, 42,* 51-78.

Porter, L., Allen, R., & Angle, H. (1981). The politics of upward influence in organizations. *Research in Organizational Behavior, 3,* 109-150.

Porter, M. (1980). *Competitive strategy: Techniques for analyzing industries and competitors.* New York: Free Press.

Powell, W. (1990). Neither market nor hierarchy: Network forms of organization. *Research in Organizational Behavior, 12,* 295-336.

President and Fellows of Harvard College. (1980). *Action planning and implementation: A manager's checklist.* No. 9-481-010. Boston: HBS Case Services.

Price, J., & Mueller, C. (1986). *Handbook of organizational measurement.* Marshfield, MA: Pitman.

Pritchard, R., Jones, S., Roth, P., Stuebing, K., & Ekeberg, S. (1989). The evaluation of an integrated approach to measuring organizational productivity. *Personnel Psychology,* 69-115.

Pritchard, R., Weiss, L., Goode, A., & Jensen, L. (1990). Measuring organizational productivity with ProMES. *National Productivity Review, 9,* 257-271.

Quinn, J. B. (1977). Strategic goals: Process and politics. *Sloan Management Review, 19,* 21-37.

Quinn, R., & Cameron, K. (1983). Organizational life cycles and shifting criteria of effectiveness: Some preliminary evidence. *Management Science, 29,* 33-51.

Ramirez, I. L., & Bartunek, J. (1989). The multiple realities and experiences of organization development consultation in health care. *Journal of Organizational Change Management, 2* (1), 40-57.

Reason, P. (1984). Is organization development possible in power cultures? In Kakabadse, A. & Parker, C. (Eds.), *Power politics and organizations: A behavioral science view* (pp. 185-202). Chichester, Eng.: Wiley.

Robbins, S. P. (1978). Conflict management and conflict resolution are not synonymous terms. *California Management Review, 21,* 67-75.

Rossi, P., & Freeman, H. (1993). *Evaluation: A systematic approach* (5th ed.). Beverly Hills, CA: Sage.

Rossi, P., & Whyte, W. F. (1983). The applied side of sociology. In H. Freeman, R. Dynes, P. Rossi, & W. F. Whyte (Eds.), *Applied sociology.* (pp. 5-31). San Francisco: Jossey-Bass.

Rousseau, D. (1990). Assessing organizational culture: The case for multiple methods. In B. Schneider (Ed.), *Climate and culture* (pp. 153-192). San Francisco: Jossey-Bass.

Rubenstein, D., & Woodman, R. (1984). Spiderman and the Burma Raiders: Collateral organization theory in action. *Journal of Applied Behavioral Science, 20,* 1-21.

Salancik, G., & Pfeffer, J. (1977). An examination of need satisfaction models of job attitudes. *Administrative Science Quarterly, 22,* 427-456.

Sandman, B. (1992). The measurement of job stress. In C. J. Cranny, P. Smith & E. Stone (Eds.), *Job satisfaction: How people feel about their jobs and how it affects their performance* (pp. 241-256). New York: Lexington Books.

Sashkin, M., & Burke, W. (1990). Understanding and assessing organizational leadership. In K. Clark & M. Clark (Eds.), *Measures of leadership* (pp. 297-325). West Orange, NJ: Leadership Library of America.

Savage, G., Nix, T., Whitehead, C., & Blair, J. (1991). Strategies for assessing and managing organizational stakeholders. *Academy of Management Executive, 5,* 61-75.

Sayles, L. (1979). *Leadership.* New York: McGraw-Hill.

Schatzman, L., & Strauss, A. (1973). *Field methods.* Englewood Cliffs, NJ: Prentice-Hall.

Schein, E. (1969). *Process consultation: Its role in organization development.* Reading, MA: Addison-Wesley.

Schein, E. (1985). *Organizational culture and leadership.* San Francisco: Jossey-Bass.

Schneider, B. (Ed.). (1990). *Climate and Culture.* San Francisco: Jossey-Bass.

Schneier, C., Shaw, D., & Beatty, R. (1992). Performance measurement and management: A tool for strategy execution. *Human Resource Management, 30,* 279-301.

Schon, D. (1983). *The reflective practitioner—How professionals think in action.* New York: Basic Books.

Schuler, R., & MacMillan, I. (1984). Gaining competitive advantage through human resource management practices. *Human Resource Management, 23,* 241-255.

Schwartz, H., & Davis, S. M. (1981). Matching corporate culture and business strategy. *Organizational Dynamics, 10* (Summer), 30-48.

Scott, J. (1991). *Social network analysis: A handbook.* Newbury Park, CA: Sage.

Seashore, S., Lawler, E., Mirvis, P., & Cammann, C. (Eds.) (1983). *Assessing organizational change.* New York: Wiley.

Selltiz, C., Wrightsman, L., & Cooke, S. (1976). *Research methods in social relations* (3rd ed.). New York: Holt, Rinehart and Winston.

Shea, G. (1986). Quality circles: The danger of bottled change. *Sloan Management Review, 26* (Spring), 33-46.

Shirom, A. (1983). Toward a theory of organizational development interventions in unionized work settings. *Human Relations, 36,* 743-764.

Shirom, A. (1993a). A diagnostic approach to labor relations in organizations. *Research in the Sociology of Organizations, 12,* 211-243.

Shirom, A. (1993b). *Toward a diagnostic model of macro-systems in the public sector: The case of Israel's health care system.* In D. Chinitz & M. Cohen (Eds.), *The changing roles of government and the market in health care systems.* Jerusalem: the JDC Brookdale Institute of Gerontology and Human Development and The State of Israel, Ministry of Health.

Smith, P. (1992). In pursuit of happiness: Why study general job satisfaction. In C. J. Cranny, P. Smith, & E. Stone (Eds.), *Job satisfaction: How people feel about their jobs and how it affects their performance* (pp. 5-20). New York: Lexington Books.

Starbuck, W., Greve, A., & Hedberg, B. (1978). Responding to crisis. *Journal of Business Administration, 9,* 111-137.

Stebbins, M. W., & Shani, A. B. (1989). Organization design: Beyond the Mafia model. *Organizational Dynamics, 17,* 18-30.

Steele, F. (1973). *Physical settings and organization development.* Reading, MA: Addison-Wesley.

Stein, B., & Kanter, E. R. (1980). Building the parallel organization: Creating mechanisms for permanent quality of work life. *Journal of Applied Behavioral Science, 16,* 371-388.

Stone, E. (1992). A critical analysis of social information processing models of job perceptions and job attitudes. In C. J. Cranny, P. Smith, & E. Stone (Eds.), *Job satisfaction: How people feel about their jobs and how it affects their performance* (pp. 21-44). New York: Lexington Books.

Strauss, A. (1987). *Qualitative analysis for social scientists.* New York: Cambridge University Press.

Strauss, G. (1976). Organization development. In R. Dubin (Ed.), *Handbook of work, organization, and society* (pp. 617-685). Chicago: Rand McNally.

Strauss, G. (1977). Managerial practices. In J. Hackman & T. Suttle (Eds.), *Improving life at work* (pp. 297-363). Santa Monica, CA: Goodyear.

Strauss, G. (1982). Workers' participation in management: An international perspective. *Research in organizational behavior, 4,* 173-265.

Sussman, G. (1990). Work groups: Autonomy, technology, and choice. In P. Goodman, L. Sproull, & Associates, *Technology and organizations* (pp. 87-108). San Francisco: Jossey-Bass.

Sutherland, J. (Ed.). (1978). *Management handbook for public administrators.* New York: Van Nostrand.

Tannenbaum, A. (1968). *Control in organizations.* New York: McGraw-Hill.

Taylor, J., & Bowers, D. (1972). *Survey of organizations: A machine scored standardized questionnaire instrument.* Ann Arbor: Institute for Social Research, University of Michigan.

Tichy, N. (1983). *Managing strategic change: Technical, political, and cultural dynamics.* New York: Wiley.

Tichy, N., & DeVanna, M. (1986). *The transformational leader.* New York: Wiley.

Tichy, N., Tushman, M., & Fombrun, C. (1980). Network analysis in organizations. In E. Lawler et al. (Eds.), *Organizational Assessment* (pp. 372-398). New York: Wiley.

Torbert, W. (1981). The role of self-study in improving managerial and institutional effectiveness. *Human Systems Management, 2,* 72-82.

Tsui, A. (1990). A multiple-constituency model of effectiveness: An empirical examination at the human resource subunit level. *Administrative Science Quarterly, 35,* 458-484.

Turner, A. (1982). Consulting is more than giving advice. *Harvard Business Review, 60,* 120-129.

Tushman, M. (1977). A political approach to organizations: A review and rationale. *Academy of Management Review, 2,* 206-216.

Tushman, M., & Nadler, D. (1978). Information processing as an integrative concept in organizational design. *Academy of Management Review, 3,* 613-624.

Tushman, M., Newman, W. & Nadler, D. (1988). Executive leadership and organizational evolution: Managing incremental and discontinuous change. In R. Kilmann, T. Covin & Associates, *Corporate transformations: Revitalizing organizations for a competitive world,* (pp.102-130). San Francisco: Jossey-Bass.

Tyson, S., Ackerman, K. F., Domsch, M., & Joynt, P. (1988). *Appraising and exploring organizations.* London: Croom Helm.

Van de Ven, A., & Chu, Y. (1989). A psychometric assessment of the Minnesota Innovation Survey. In A. Van de Ven, H. Angle, & M. Poole (Eds.), *Research on the management of innovation.* New York: Harper and Row.

Van de Ven, A., & Drazin, R. (1985). The concept of fit in contingency theory. *Research in organizational behavior, 7,* 333-365.

Van de Ven, A., & Ferry, D. (1980). *Measuring and assessing organizations.* New York: Wiley.

Van de Ven, A., & Walker, A. (1984). The dynamics of interorganizational coordination. *Administrative Science Quarterly, 29,* 598-621.

Van Maanen, J. (Ed.). (1979). Qualitative methodology. *Administrative Science Quarterly, 24,* 519-712.

Walton, R. (1975). Quality of working life: What is it? *Sloan Management Review, 15,* 11-21.

Walton, R., & Dutton, J. (1969). The management of interdepartmental conflict: A model and review. *Administrative Science Quarterly, 14,* 73-84.

Walton, R., & Warwick, D. (1973). The ethics of organization development. *Journal of Applied Behavioral Science, 9,* 681-698.

Webb, E., Campbell, D., Schwartz, R., & Seechrest, L. (1966). *Unobtrusive measures: Non-reactive research in the social sciences.* Chicago: Rand McNally.

Weick, K. (1979). *The social psychology of organizing* (2nd ed.). Reading, MA: Addison-Wesley.

Weick, K. (1985). Systematic observation methods. In G. Lindzey & E. Aronson (Eds.), *Handbook of Social Psychology* (3rd ed.), Vol. 2 (pp. 567-634). Reading, MA: Addison-Wesley.

Weisbord, M. (1978). *Organizational diagnosis: A workbook of theory and practice.* Reading, MA: Addison-Wesley.

Weitzel, W., & Jonsson, E. (1991). Reversing the downward spiral: Lessons from W. T. Grant and Sears Roebuck. *Academy of Management Executive, 5*(3), 7-22.

Whetten, D. (1987). Organizational growth and decline processes. *Annual Review of Sociology, 13,* 335-358.

Wildavsky, A. (1972). The self-evaluating organization. *Public Administration Review, 32,* 509-520.

Zald, M., & Berger, M. (1978). Social movements in organizations: Coup d'etat, insurgency, and mass movements. *American Journal of Sociology, 83,* 823-861.

Zammuto, R. F. (1984). A comparison of multiple constituency models of organizational effectiveness. *Academy of Management Review, 9,* 606-616.

Author Index

Subject Index

About the Author

Michael I. Harrison is an Associate Professor in the Department of Sociology and Anthropology at Bar-Ilan University in Ramat-Gan, Israel, and director of its Graduate Program in the Sociology of Organizations. He received his doctorate in sociology from the University of Michigan in 1972 and was a faculty member at State University of New York, Stony Brook, between 1970 and 1974. He joined the faculty at Bar-Ilan in 1974 and has served as department chairperson. He has also been a Visiting Associate Professor in the Department of Organization Studies/Human Resources Management at the School of Management at Boston College and a visiting scholar at the Graduate School of Business of Harvard University. Professor Harrison has worked as a consultant and conducted research in businesses, service and government organizations, worker-managed cooperatives, and voluntary groups. His research concentrates on organizations and the professions. He is engaged in a study of the impacts of health system reforms on physicians and other health professionals in five nations. He is also writing a book with Professor Aryeh Shirom on models for organizational diagnosis and assessment, to be published by Sage.